3-

pure vegetarian

Paul Gayler

pure vegetarian

modern and stylish vegetarian cooking

photography by Gus Filgate

Kyle Books

To all those who love food—
a constant source of joy

All recipes serve 4 unless otherwise stated

This edition published in 2006 by Kyle Books
An imprint of Kyle Cathie Limited
www.kylecathie.com

Distributed by National Book Network
4501 Frobes Blvd., Suite 200
Lanham, MD 20706
Phone: (301) 459 3366 Fax: (301) 429 5746

ISBN 1 904920 40 3
ISBN (13-digit) 978 1 904920 40 3

Editor Sophie Allen
Designer Vanessa Courtier
Photographer Gus Filgate
Home economist Linda Tubby
Stylist Penny Markham
Proofreader Stephanie Horner
Indexer Alex Corrin
Americanizer Adèle Linderholm
Production by Sha Huxtable and Alice Holloway

Gayler, Paul.
Pure Vegetarian: Modern and Stylish Vegetarian Cooking/
Paul Gayler.
1. Cookery, Vegetarian.
Library of Congress Control Number: 2006924046

 1 2 3 4 5 01 02 03 04 05

Colour Reproduction by SC International
Printed and bound in China by
C & C Offset Printing Company Ltd

Contents

Introduction 6

Predinner finger foods 8

Appetizers 20

Soups 50

Salads 68

Pasta and grains 88

Main dishes 126

Pastry 158

Desserts 176

Sauces and broths 188

Index 190

Conversion tables 192

Introduction

I wrote my first book, *Virtually Vegetarian*, over ten years ago. A celebration of vegetables and vegetarian cooking, it placed vegetables firmly center stage. It was the beginning of the trend towards healthier eating and healthier living, with the emphasis placed on eating a good, balanced, vegetable-based diet and reducing the consumption of meat. Looking back, I suppose it was quite radical. When I started cooking professionally, it was hard, if not impossible, to find a decent vegetarian meal. So-called top restaurants concentrated on the main course—meat—and never the vegetarian option. When I became head chef at one of London's most expensive restaurants, I was happy to cater for meat eaters and vegetarians alike. Other chefs often asked me why I bothered. After all, vegetarians didn't want to eat at such grand establishments, did they? They were just a fanatical bunch who didn't have enough to worry about! I saw it differently, however. Why shouldn't vegetarian dishes be interesting and imaginative?

Even nowadays, it is not unusual for high-profile chefs to talk contemptuously about vegetarians, saying they don't appreciate good food. But I have never considered them difficult to cater for. They are just customers who, for one reason or another, have decided to forsake meat and fish in their diet. Think about it for a moment. If you were to stay in a hotel and be served pancakes and bacon for breakfast, a BLT for lunch, and bacon and eggs for dinner, wouldn't you feel just a little aggrieved? Isn't that how a vegetarian might feel when faced with yet another offering of the ubiquitous omelette, vegetarian lasagne, or nut loaf?

I believe chefs are missing a great opportunity when they neglect to cater imaginatively for vegetarians. In recent years there has been a renewed interest in vegetarianism. While certain cultural and religious groups have practiced it for centuries, now an increasing number of people are adopting it for a variety of reasons, whether economic, humanitarian, or simply for better health. Following a vegetarian way of life is now far more acceptable than it once was—even, should I say, fashionable. It is worth remembering that roughly 45 percent of the population have reduced their meat intake by choice. In my experience, putting an interesting vegetarian option on the menu appeals to a large number of nonvegetarians too.

This is my third book on vegetarian food and I have spent twenty years catering for vegetarians at the highest level. Yet I am still a meat eater, and as such I welcome the idea that everyone can enjoy vegetarian dishes. I don't believe in fad cuisines or diet regimes, simply in good food. My greatest wish is that vegetarian cuisine will one day be on an equal footing with meat and fish cooking. Great cooking is all about taste, and I firmly believe that you can achieve complex, refined flavors in vegetable dishes, as in any other kind. On a recent trip to Italy, my family and I enjoyed some wonderful vegetable dishes in restaurants—ones that sat proudly alongside meat and fish options but were not labeled vegetarian. It was simply no big deal that they didn't contain meat.

The movement towards a greener cuisine has long been coming, and I'd like to feel I've been a little instrumental in its progress. I persevered for many years in creating what I believe in. When I started to come up with vegetarian menu ideas back in 1985, the overriding challenge was to overcome the image of bland, uninspiring dishes such as stews, bakes, and raw salads, which generally took so much time to make and gave so little pleasure in return. I wanted to produce vibrant, exciting meals, full of variety, color, flavor, and texture. Mine is a constantly evolving, progressive style of cooking, heavily shaped by two very different influences: classic French techniques, and my fascination for flavors from the Mediterranean and the Middle and Far East. This book reflects my thirst for knowledge, my inspiration from cuisines around the world, and my desire to see vegetarian cuisine become more mainstream by the day. With the huge variety of vegetarian ingredients now available, learning to cook without meat and fish doesn't mean reinventing the wheel; it just takes a little care and thought to achieve great tastes and textures.

In France many chefs are now championing vegetables, Alain Passard and Pierre Gagnaire, for example. Has their decision to embrace vegetarian cooking coincided with growing fears about the safety of the meat supply in Europe? I think not; more likely they are seizing the opportunity to inspire menus with a seasonal approach. The same can be applied to the U.S.A., where my friend, Charlie Trotter, the great chef from Chicago, continues to break the boundaries every day. These chefs treat vegetables with the kind of reverence and respect normally given to lobster or foie gras.

I hope you will find all the recipes in this book enticing and accessible. Most of them are simple to cook, although some are slightly more sophisticated and require a little more effort. You may have to search for one or two ingredients, but this is a way to experience new flavors. You will find no tempeh, no seitan, and just a few recipes for tofu, since I am not an avid lover of them. Although I am not vegetarian, the recipes respect those who choose to be so and I hope you enjoy cooking and eating them. They celebrate the extraordinary bounty of vegetarian cuisine, which has been transformed over the last twenty years from a gastronomic wilderness to a mainstream way of life that all can enjoy.

Bon Appetit!

Cooking with the seasons

From the first crisp spears of spring asparagus, tender carrots, and fava beans, to the sun-ripened tomatoes and zucchini of summer, from the jewel-colored pumpkins and squashes of fall to earthier winter favorites such as parsnips and crisp celery, the opportunities for rich and varied vegetable dishes throughout the year are endless.

So what does "eating seasonally" mean? Simply that vegetables usually taste best and are at their most nutritious when they have been grown at the time that Nature intended (rather than cultivated in artificial conditions) and are eaten as soon as possible after harvesting (rather than kept in storage or flown halfway around the world). This way you not only get the best and freshest ingredients to work with, but pay less for them, since prices remain low with the seasonal bumper crops.

Vegetables, herbs, and fruits in season are so vibrantly flavored that even the simplest preparation yields great results. I find it rather sad that our children rarely, if at all, get the opportunity to experience the taste of real food, such as a sun-warmed strawberry straight from the plant, freshly dug carrots or an apple plucked from the tree. Unfortunately it is now so easy for us to forget about the seasons when we eat. Most supermarkets carry produce that looks and tastes the same all year round They claim that this is what customers want, but what's the point if they lack flavor?

However, on a brighter note small producers have fought back over the past ten years. There has been an upsurge in farm stores, farmers' markets, and home delivery vegetable boxes, which enable us to purchase wonderful, lovingly grown seasonal ingredients. Support these small businesses at every opportunity to ensure their survival in this world of competitive supermarket monopolies. You will find they often carry seasonal produce that is not available in supermarkets.

A brief explanation of vegetarian types

Ovo-lacto Vegetarians eliminate animal consumption in its entirety but allow the inclusion of eggs (ovo) and dairy (lacto) products. This allows a wide variety of choices for the consumer and the cook.

Lacto Vegetarians prefer not to eat eggs but base their diet around vegetables, fruits, nuts, seeds, and some milk and milk based products. It is a popular style of eating, especially in Far Eastern countries.

Vegans avoid all products of animal origin, including eggs, dairy products and sometimes honey. Catering for vegans can be more challenging, but with proper planning and forethought it is possible to come up with a good and varied menu.

Semivegetarians are seen as illegitimate by true vegetarians since they, through choice, include far more vegetarian meals in their diet but still occasionally eat fish, seafood, and poultry, especially chicken. Most have eliminated red meat. Can we soon expect to see the pesce vegetarian (fish eating) and the pollo vegetarian (chicken eating)? It can't be long!

Fruitarians (Microbiotic) are perhaps the most extreme of all. They consume only fruits! But this does include berries, nuts, seeds and vegetable fruits such as tomatoes, cucumbers and olives. Generally, raw fruits are preferred to cooked, thereby retaining all the vitamins, minerals, and natural enzymes. Some fruitarians opt to eat grains to add variety. It's growing in popularity in the U.S.A. but in the U.K. it has not really taken off. Medical experts say that this form of eating simply cannot provide all the nutrients needed for a healthy lifestyle.

RAW eating

Rawish is the consumption of unprocessed, preferably organic, whole, plant based foods that have never been cooked. It's ranked as one of the seven most popular diets in the world—some thirty new raw food restaurants have sprouted up (excuse the pun!) in the U.S.A. and I recently noticed the first raw food restaurant in London—but is it just another celebrity fashion statement, or a way of life for many to come?

Raw foods include fruits, vegetables, nuts, seeds, grains, sprouting legumes, dried fruits, seaweeds, freshly pressed juices, and purified water. They are believed to provide optimal nutrition for the body, since they contain more essential enzymes than cooked foods. Enthusiasts believe that enzymes are the life force of any food and offer numerous health benefits—improved digestion, sustained energy levels, maintaining a steady weight, reducing heart disease—all in all, a general way of feeling better about ourselves. When food is cooked, it is heated above 116°F, the temperature at which natural enzymes are destroyed. The only "cooking" in a raw food diet is done in a hydrator, which dries food via hot air blowing at a temperature below 116°F.

Following a raw diet can be time-consuming: Sprouting seeds and grains, soaking nuts, drying fruits, and juicing vegetables and fruits. And medical experts are skeptical about the benefits, claiming that it can be unhealthy, restrictive, and limited. Many users eat only 75 percent raw food while lightly cooking the rest. But this is not a good compromise—mixing a little cooked food with the raw produces acid in the stomach, creating digestive problems.

Although I find this diet interesting from a culinary standpoint, I have yet to be convinced of its benefits. I have included some simple raw dishes (symbolized by RAW in the title) that don't involve the use of dehydrators. They give you a feel for the freshness of this type of eating and the opportunity to make up your own mind.

Predinner finger foods

In these times of increased home entertaining, it seems to be the norm to serve a little nibble or two along with predinner drinks. Whether served hot or cold, they are an impressive way to start off an evening. A good tip to remember is to keep them small, simple, and easy to prepare and eat. In this chapter, I hope that you will discover some delightful and imaginative dishes that can be prepared with confidence and are guaranteed to whet the appetite.

Steamed oriental buns

These delicate Malaysian-style buns are best made fresh, although they can be frozen raw and baked when needed. You may wish to serve some extra-sweet chili sauce on the side as a dip.

for the dough

3 cups "00" flour

1 tablespoon baking powder

1 tablespoon superfine sugar

1 tablespoon vegetable oil

3/4 cup warm water

for the filling

2 teaspoons sesame oil

1 pound shiitake mushrooms, chopped

1/2 garlic clove, crushed

1 tablespoon sugar

4 tablespoons peanut butter

1 tablespoon hoisin sauce

2 tablespoons sweet chili sauce

2 tablespoons chopped fresh cilantro

makes 16 buns

For the dough, sift the dry ingredients into a bowl, stir in the oil and water, mix to a soft dough, and shape into a ball. Knead on a lightly floured surface for about 3–4 minutes until smooth and pliable. Return to the bowl, cover with a dish towel and leave to stand for 10–15 minutes.

For the filling, heat the sesame oil in a wok or small skillet, add the mushrooms and garlic, and stir-fry for 2–3 minutes. Add the remaining ingredients, mix well together, and cook until the mixture is thick and sticky in texture. Remove to a bowl and leave to cool.

Roll out the dough and, using a 3 inch cookie cutter, cut out sixteen circles. Flatten each circle with the palm of your hand to form thin circles (about 3/4 inch thick). Place a good tablespoon of the mushroom filling in the center of each circle, gather up the edges, and twist firmly to secure the filling. Place the buns (gathered-side up) onto a foil or paper lined bamboo steamer, making sure the buns are not touching. Place over a wok or pan of simmering water for 15 minutes or until firm. Serve warm.

Cajun mozzarella and ricotta fritters

Adding cajun spices to the cheese mixture really gives the fritters a lift
and is an ideal way to get the gastric juices flowing.

14 ounces ricotta cheese, well drained

$1/2$ teaspoon garlic powder

$1/2$ teaspoon cayenne

1 teaspoon smoked paprika (or paprika)

1 tablespoon chopped fresh oregano leaves

1 tablespoon fresh thyme leaves

$1^1/3$ cups dried white breadcrumbs

$1/2$ pound buffalo mozzarella, patted dry and
* cut into $1/2$ inch dice*

$1/2$ cup all-purpose flour

2 free-range eggs, beaten

$2/3$ cup fine cornmeal (polenta)

vegetable oil for deep-frying

salt and cracked black pepper

for the Virgin Mary dip

1 teaspoon Worcestershire sauce

$1/2$ cup tomato ketchup

drop of Tabasco sauce

1 teaspoon creamed horseradish

salt and freshly ground black pepper

makes 16 fritters

Place the drained ricotta in a bowl and add the garlic powder, spices and fresh herbs; season well with salt and cracked black pepper. Stir in half the breadcrumbs, then add the dried mozzarella. Divide the mixture into sixteen small balls, place on a plate and refrigerate for 1 hour to firm up.

For the dip, combine all the ingredients together in a bowl and season to taste.

Remove the cheese balls from the fridge, pass them through the flour, then into the beaten eggs, and then into a mixture of the remaining breadcrumbs and the fine cornmeal. Roll them individually in the palm of your hand to obtain good round shapes.

Heat the vegetable oil to 350°F and add the fritters a few at a time, being careful not to overcrowd the pan. Deep-fry for 1–2 minutes until golden, remove and drain on kitchen paper. Pierce each ball with a toothpick and place on a serving dish with some Virgin Mary dip on the side.

Mini eggplant egg rolls

These egg rolls are extremely tasty and the ideal finger food with drinks.
They can be made in advance and frozen to take a little stress out of
entertaining. Serve with soy sauce.

4 tablespoons sunflower oil

2 teaspoons sesame oil

2 medium-size eggplants, cut into $^1/2$ inch dice

1 shallot, finely chopped

1 small garlic clove, crushed

1 tablespoon sweet chili sauce

2 tablespoons Indonesian soy sauce (kecap manis)

2 tablespoons chopped fresh cilantro

12 egg roll wrappers

4 tablespoons peanut oil

salt and freshly ground black pepper

makes 12 rolls

Heat the sunflower oil and sesame oil in a skillet over a moderate heat, add the diced eggplant, shallot, and garlic and stir-fry for 5–6 minutes until golden and tender. Place into a bowl and leave to cool. When cool, add the chili sauce, kecap manis and chopped cilantro; season to taste.

Lay the egg roll wrappers out on a work surface and place an equal amount of eggplant filling at one end of each wrapper. Roll up tightly, folding in the sides to secure the filling. Brush the end of each wrapper with a little water to seal.

Heat the peanut oil in a skillet and fry the egg rolls for 4–5 minutes, turning them regularly until golden all over. Drain on paper towels and serve with soy sauce.

Mini tortilla wraps

These little wraps of flour tortillas are packed with flavor and have been served as vegetarian canapés at The Lanesborough for more years than I care to remember.

2 tablespooons unsalted butter

1 small red chili, deseeded and finely chopped

5 ounces baby spinach, washed and well drained

1/2 cup cooked black beans, lightly crushed

1 small ripe mango, peeled and cut into 1cm dice

3/4 cup freshly grated vegetarian cheddar cheese

2 flour tortillas

1/2 cup sour cream

salt and freshly ground black pepper

makes 12 mini wraps

Melt the butter in a skillet, throw in the chili and spinach, and cook over a high heat for 1 minute. Add the lightly crushed black beans and mango and toss the whole mix together; season to taste. Remove from the heat, add the cheese, and mix well. Set aside.

Heat another large skillet and, when hot, add the tortillas one at a time and toast them on both sides for 10–15 seconds until lightly charred. Lay out the tortillas on a flat surface, fill each one with equal quantities of the filling, then roll them up tightly into wraps. Trim the ends off the tortillas and then cut each one into six small equal wraps. Serve with the sour cream.

Warm mini cocktail sandwiches

Based on the English tea sandwich, these tasty bite-size morsels come from further afield. They combine freshness and simplicity for serving with predinner drinks. And they can be prepared beforehand and cooked when needed.

Tapenade with semidry tomato toasts

Tapenade is an olive paste that can be made easily, but you can find some delicious ready-made versions in good delicatessens.

$^1/_2$ stick unsalted butter, softened

2 tablespoons arugula, roughly chopped

4 slices of white sandwich bread

2 tablespoons tapenade

4 tablespoons semidry tomatoes, drained and dried

$^1/_3$ cup fontina (or emmental) cheese, grated

2 tablespoons olive oil

salt and freshly ground black pepper

makes 12 squares

Mix the butter and arugula and season lightly. Spread the arugula butter on both sides of each bread slice. Spread a layer of tapenade onto two of the slices of bread. Top with semidry tomatoes, covering the whole surface. Scatter over the fontina cheese, then close up the sandwiches with the other two pieces of bread, pressing down gently to make them compact.

Heat the olive oil in a skillet over a moderate heat and fry the sandwiches for about 2 minutes on each side until golden all over. Remove and drain on paper towels. Using a sharp knife, remove the crusts and cut each sandwich into six small squares. Serve immediately.

Crushed artichoke and chèvre pesto toasts

If you can, buy your artichoke hearts from a good Italian delicatessen for that superior flavor.

¹/2 stick unsalted butter, softened
4 slices of white sandwich bread
4 marinated artichoke hearts, drained and dried
2 tablespoons soft chèvre
1 tablespoon pesto (homemade or bought)
1 teaspoon chopped fresh oregano
2 tablespoons freshly grated castelli vegetalia
  (parmesan-style cheese)
2 tablespoons olive oil
salt and freshly ground black pepper

makes 12 squares

Spread the butter on both sides of each bread slice. In a bowl, break up the marinated artichokes with a fork. Add the chèvre, pesto, and oregano; season well to taste.

Carefully spread out the mixture onto two of the buttered slices, then close up the sandwiches with the other two pieces of bread, pressing down gently to make them compact. Sprinkle them both liberally all over with grated parmesan.

Heat the olive oil in a skillet over a moderate heat and fry the sandwiches for about 2 minutes on each side until golden all over. Remove and drain on paper towels. Using a sharp knife, remove the crusts and cut each sandwich into six small squares. Serve immediately.

Wild mushroom and taleggio croque monsieurs

Taleggio is a wonderful Italian cheese that goes so well with wild mushrooms.

4 tablespoons olive oil
¹/4 pound assorted wild mushrooms, cleaned and sliced
1 garlic clove, crushed
1 tablespoon chopped fresh flat-leaf parsley
¹/2 stick unsalted butter, softened
4 slices of white sandwich bread
2 ounces taleggio cheese, thinly sliced
salt and freshly ground black pepper

makes 12 squares

Heat half the olive oil in a skillet over a moderate heat, add the mushrooms and garlic, and fry until golden and tender. Add the parsley and season well to taste. Remove and leave to cool.

Spread the butter on both sides of each bread slice. Divide the mushrooms equally and place onto two slices of the bread. Top the mushrooms with slices of the taleggio, then close up the sandwiches with the other two slices of bread, pressing down gently to make them compact.

Heat the remaining oil in another skillet, add the sandwiches, and fry for 2–3 minutes on each side until golden all over. Remove and drain on paper towels. Using a sharp knife, remove the crusts and cut each sandwich into six small squares. Serve immediately.

Cream cheese, beet, and truffle tarts

The use of creamy cheese and sweet beets is a particular favorite of mine because it is relatively cheap, easy to prepare, and looks beautiful.

1 pound prepared short pastry

2 medium-size roasted beets (see page 77)

1 teaspoon balsamic vinegar

2 tablespoons maple syrup

1/4 pound good quality cream cheese

2 tablespoons snipped fresh chives (plus more for garnishing)

1 tablespoon truffle oil

salt and freshly ground black pepper

12 mini-tartlet pans

makes 12 tarts

Preheat the oven to 375°F. Roll out the pastry very thinly and, using a 2 inch cookie cutter, cut out twelve circles of pastry. Line twelve tartlet pans with the circles and cook in the oven for 10 minutes until golden. Leave to cool. (These may be prepared in advance and stored in an airtight container.)

Cut the beets into small dice and place in a pan with the vinegar and maple syrup. Cook over a low heat for 4–5 minutes so that they become lightly caramelized and have a sweet and sour flavor. Remove and leave to cool.

Mix the cream cheese with the chives and season to taste.

Fill each tartlet with cream cheese, then top with a spoonful of beets. Drizzle a little truffle oil over each tartlet, garnish with some snipped chives, and serve.

Appetizers

Although all constituents of a great meal are significant, one must never forget the importance of a well-prepared appetizer. It must be beautiful to look at and ultimately light and flavorful, while leaving room for the dishes to follow. Inevitably it sets the tone of what's to come, but more importantly it stimulates the palate and entices and delights the diner. Creating interesting appetizers opens up a world of culinary adventures—all it takes is a little imagination.

Vegetables à la grecque
with avocado cheese and herb-scented juices

A light and tasty vegetable dish, simply presented in the Greek style, accompanied with a fragrant herb sauce made from the cooking juices—ideal for the summertime.

for the avocado cheese

1/2 avocado, preferably Haas variety
1/4 pound feta cheese
juice of 1/2 lemon
salt and freshly ground black pepper

4 tablespoons white wine vinegar
1 garlic clove, crushed
juice of 1 lemon
1 teaspoon coriander seeds, crushed
sprig of fresh thyme
8 tablespoons olive oil
1/2 pound baby zucchini, halved lengthwise
16 green asparagus tips, peeled and trimmed
4 white asparagus tips, peeled and trimmed
4 teaspoons fresh flat-leaf parsley leaves
2 tablespoons fresh basil leaves
3 tablespoons fresh celery leaves
salt and freshly ground black pepper

For the avocado cheese, place the avocado flesh and cheese in a food processor and blend to a smooth paste. Remove to a bowl, add the lemon juice, and season to taste. Cover the bowl with plastic wrap and refrigerate until required.

Heat 3/4 cup water with the vinegar, garlic, lemon juice, coriander seeds, and thyme in a pan, bring to a boil and simmer for 15 minutes. Add half the oil. Add the zucchini and asparagus and cook until just tender, retaining a little crunch to them. Remove and leave to cool, reserving the cooking liquid.

Place the parsley, basil, and celery leaves in a food processor and blend, adding enough of the cooking liquid to form a light purée. Add the remaining olive oil, blend again, remove, and season to taste.

Pour a little of the sauce on each serving plate, add the cooked vegetables and top with a quenelle of avocado cheese (using a spoon or ice-cream scoop). Garnish with the coriander seeds and thyme leaves from the cooking liquid.

Haloumi tandoori
with carrot pachadi

I am a great lover of the foods of Asia—vibrant and flavor-packed dishes that excite the palate and all the senses. The haloumi cheese skewers are more at home in Central Europe than India, but it really works well with the tandoori spices.

for the haloumi marinade

2 garlic cloves, crushed

2 tablespoons chopped fresh cilantro

2 shallots, chopped

2 red bell peppers, deseeded and chopped

juice of 1 lime

1 teaspoon paprika

2 tablespoons tandoori paste

1 pound haloumi cheese

little olive oil

for the carrot pachadi

4 tablespoons olive oil

12 curry leaves

pinch of black mustard seeds

1 garlic clove

pinch of salt

1 small red chili, deseeded and finely chopped

juice of 1 lemon

1 large carrot, peeled and finely shredded

1 red onion, thinly sliced

4 wooden or bamboo skewers
(soaked in water for 24 hours)

For the haloumi marinade, place all the ingredients except the tandoori paste in a food processor and blend until smooth. Add the paste, blend again, and transfer into a large bowl. Cut the haloumi into large blocks, place in a bowl, and toss well with the marinade. Cover with plastic wrap and refrigerate overnight.

Thread the haloumi onto the wooden skewers to form a kebab. Heat a little olive oil in a large skillet or alternatively in a broiler pan over a moderate heat. Cook the kebabs for 1–2 minutes on each side. (Do not overcook them because haloumi can become hard when overcooked.)

While they cook, heat the 4 tablespoons of olive oil in a small skillet over a moderate heat and fry the curry leaves and mustard seeds for 20–30 seconds.

Crush the garlic in a mortar with a little salt and chili. Add the lemon juice, curry leaves, and mustard seeds. Transfer to a bowl, add the shredded carrot and onion, and toss well together. Serve with the kebabs.

PG TIPS   I also occasionally serve some thick yogurt on the side, which I think goes well with this dish.

Seaweed daikon wraps
with ginger and sesame dipping sauce—RAW

A simple and healthy raw dish of marinated shredded vegetables
wrapped in thin white radish slices. They are star attractions in
Vietnamese homes and can be made with all kinds of fillings. Yuzu is an
unusual citrus fruit with a flavor that is a cross between a tangerine and a
lime. Replace with fresh lime juice if you need to.

1 white radish (daikon)

2 tablespoons maple syrup

1 ounce raw cashews, finely chopped

2 tablespoons yuzu juice (or lime juice)

1 avocado, halved, stoned and cut into $^1/_3$ inch dice

*1 ounce hijiki (or wakame) seaweed, soaked in hot water
    for 15–20 minutes, drained and dried*

$^1/_2$ cucumber, deseeded and thinly shredded

1 red bell pepper, deseeded and thinly shredded

1 carrot, peeled and thinly sliced

1 small mango, peeled and thinly shredded

2 tablespoons fresh cilantro leaves

2 tablespoons fresh mint leaves

2 tablespoons fresh basil leaves

4 tablespoons purple shiso cress (if available)

salt and freshly ground black pepper

for the dipping sauce
5 tablespoons rice wine vinegar

2 tablespoons soy sauce

*1 stick of lemongrass, outer casing discarded,
    finely chopped*

1 tablespoon pickled ginger, chopped, juice reserved

2 tablespoons ginger juice (from above)

1 tablespoon peanut oil

1 tablespoon sesame oil

1 tablespoon yuzu juice (or lime juice)

salt and freshly ground black pepper

makes 12 wraps

Peel the white radish and slice very thinly lengthwise using a kitchen mandolin (a
similar result can be achieved using a broad-bladed swivel-headed vegetable peeler)
and set aside.

   In a large bowl, mix together the maple syrup, cashews, and yuzu juice. Add the
avocado, seaweed, vegetables, mango, and herbs, except the shiso cress, and toss
gently together; season to taste.

   To assemble the rolls, trim the radish slices to $^3/_4$ inch strips in length. Lay two
strips alongside each other, slightly overlapping, place a scoop of the mixture at one
end. Add the shiso cress on top, then roll up firmly to form neat rolls. Place on a
large plate. The mixture should make twelve wraps in total. Keep chilled.

   For the dipping sauce, combine the vinegar, soy sauce, lemongrass, ginger, and
juice in a food processor. With the machine running, slowly drizzle in the oils and
yuzu or lime juice and adjust the seasoning.

   Place the wraps on a serving plate (cut them in half if you prefer) and serve with
the dipping sauce alongside.

PG TIPS   Another great dipping sauce for these wraps can be made by simply
blending together 1 avocado with 1 chopped green onion and the juice of half a
lemon. Then add 1 tablespoon of rice wine vinegar, 4 tablespoons of coconut milk,
and blend to a purée. Remove and fold in with 1 tablespoon of sweet chili sauce
before serving.

Stuffed zucchini flowers

with chickpeas, new potatoes, and lemon olive oil

Chefs eagerly await the summer and the arrival of the first zucchini flowers to adorn their tables. If you are not lucky enough to grow your own or know someone who does, they can be found in specialty stores or country farm stores.

12 zucchini blossoms (female, small zucchini attached)
1 tablespoon olive oil
1 small onion, chopped
1 garlic clove, crushed
1 red bell pepper, roasted, deseeded, and chopped
1 cup chickpea flour (gram flour)
1 cup cooked chickpeas (canned are fine)
1 teaspoon chopped fresh rosemary
1 litre vegetable oil
salt and freshly ground black pepper

for the batter

1 free-range egg
$^1/2$ cup all-purpose flour (plus a little extra for coating)
4 tablespoons cold water

for the salad

$^3/4$ pound new potatoes, scrubbed
3 tablespoons watercress, leaves only
3 tablespoons arugula leaves
2 hardboiled free-range eggs, shelled

for the lemon olive oil

$^1/4$ cup extra-virgin olive oil
2 ounces pitted black olives
zest and juice of $^1/2$ lemon

serves 4–6

Firstly clean the zucchini by gently washing the flowers and drying the outside.

For the stuffing, heat the olive oil in a pan, add the onion, garlic, and pepper and cook over a low heat for 4–5 minutes until soft. In a separate pan bring to a boil $^3/4$ cup water, pour in the chickpea flour and stir until smooth, lower the heat and cook for 2–3 minutes. In a food processor blend the chickpeas with the onion, garlic, and pepper to a coarse paste. Add the chickpea flour mixture and rosemary and season. Leave to cool.

For the batter, beat the eggs in a bowl, stir in the flour, then gradually add the water to make a smooth consistency. Set aside.

For the salad, cook the potatoes in plenty of boiling salted water until tender. Drain and leave to cool to room temperature. Slice the potatoes and place in a bowl, add the watercress and arugula. Chop the egg whites and pass the yolks through a sieve and add to the salad. Set aside.

Fill the zucchini flowers with the chickpea mixture and twist the ends to secure the inner filling. Heat the vegetable oil to 325°F. Dip the flowers into a little flour, then into the batter, and fry in the hot oil for about 1–2 minutes until golden brown. Drain on the paper towels.

For the lemon olive oil, mix all the ingredients together in a bowl. Toss the salad with the dressing and place onto four individual plates. Place the zucchini flowers on top and serve.

Poached egg on potato muffins
with watercress hollandaise

Spring heralds the arrival of vitamin-packed watercress, hailed today as a superhero among salad leaves. However, the use of watercress in hot dishes should never be overlooked—here it makes an interesting addition to the well-loved hollandaise sauce. A great dish that can be enjoyed for breakfast, lunch, or brunch.

5 tablespoons unsalted butter

2 small leeks, trimmed and thinly shredded

1 1/2 cups hot mashed potato (made with floury potatoes)

1/4 cup freshly grated castelli vegetalia (parmesan-style cheese)

1 free-range egg, beaten

1/2 cup all-purpose flour (plus a little extra for coating)

4 tablespoons vegetable oil

2 tablespoons vinegar

4 large free-range eggs

watercress to garnish (optional)

1 tablespoon truffle oil

salt and freshly ground black pepper

for the watercress hollandaise

3 large free-range egg yolks at room temperature

juice of 1/2 lemon

2 ounces watercress, leaves only

2 sticks unsalted butter

salt and freshly ground black pepper

Melt 3 tablespoons butter in a pan, add the leeks and cook over a low heat for 8–10 minutes or until tender.

Place the hot mashed potato in a bowl, beat in the remaining butter and the cheese, and season well. Beat in the egg and flour. Divide the potato mixture into four equal portions and, with floured hands, form the portions into balls and then make an indentation in the center of each ball. Place a good spoonful of the leeks into each indentation, then reform the balls to totally enclose the filling. Flatten each ball to make a flat cake about 1 inch deep, then coat each one in a little flour. Set aside.

For the hollandaise, place the egg yolks, 2 tablespoons of water, the lemon juice, watercress, and a little salt and pepper in a food processor and blend until just combined. Heat the butter in a pan to just under boiling point. With the motor running, gently pour in the butter through the funnel at the top, leaving the milky residues behind—the sauce should be creamy and thick. Adjust the seasoning to taste and keep warm.

Heat the vegetable oil in a skillet over a moderate heat and fry the potato muffins for 3–4 minutes on each side until golden. Meanwhile poach the eggs.

Bring 3 cups water with the vinegar to a boil. Reduce the heat, crack in the eggs, two at a time, and simmer gently for 2–3 minutes or until the eggs are just set but still a little soft. Carefully remove them from the water with a slotted spoon and drain well on paper towels.

Place the potato muffins on four plates, carefully top each with a poached egg, a grinding of black pepper, and a spoonful or two of watercress hollandaise. Garnish with the watercress, if using, then finally drizzle over a little truffle oil.

Pan-roasted asparagus
with truffled eggs sunnyside up

If you are ever lucky enough to have a freshly dug white Piedmont truffle at hand, then this is the dish for it. The combination of butter-fried egg, asparagus, and truffle is a dish of simplicity but utmost sophistication. White truffles are found from late fall to early winter—they are extremely expensive and highly regarded.

for the gremolata
1/4 stick unsalted butter
1 1/3 cups fresh white breadcrumbs
2 tablespoons chopped fresh flat-leaf parsley
1 tablespoon freshly grated castelli vegetalia
   (parmesan-style cheese)

24 fresh green asparagus, peeled and trimmed
3 tablespoons unsalted butter
4 large free-range eggs
1 small white truffle
salt and freshly cracked black pepper

For the gremolata, heat the butter in a pan and, when foaming, add the breadcrumbs and parsley, and cook until lightly golden and toasted. Add the castelli vegetalia, remove, and leave to cool.

   Cook the asparagus in boiling salted water for 3–4 minutes or until tender (according to their size), remove and drain well. In a small nonstick skillet, melt the butter and fry the eggs. Place the asparagus onto four serving plates and top with a fried egg. Season with salt and freshly cracked black pepper. Sprinkle over the gremolata. Finally shave the white truffle over the top and serve immediately.

PG TIPS   You could use a teaspoon of white truffle oil (which is far less expensive!) and drizzle it over the eggs instead of the fresh white truffle—your pocket will be better for it but the flavor won't, I'm afraid.

Rosemary-broiled chèvre

with warm apricot relish and pistachio oil

Canned apricots are best for this relish because they are cooked for a
short time to retain their natural flavors. It has a tangy sweet and sour
flavor, which works wonderfully with the taste of rosemary-broiled cheese.

4 tablespoons heavy cream

1 teaspoon fresh rosemary leaves, roughly chopped

4 small round chèvre (e.g. crottin chavignol)

2 small crisp bread rolls, each cut into 4 thin
*   slices lengthwise*

extra-virgin olive oil for brushing

2 ounces fresh buckler leaf sorrel or watercress

for the apricot relish

1 small onion, finely chopped

4 tablespoons white wine vinegar

2 tablespoons brown sugar

1 pound canned apricots, chopped and juice reserved

2 tablespoons raisins, soaked until plump in warm
*   water, drained*

for the pistachio oil

$^1/2$ cup good quality very green pistachio nuts

$^1/2$ cup extra-virgin olive oil

Preheat a broiler to its highest setting. Place the cream and chopped rosemary in a
small bowl and lightly whip with a small whisk or fork until it begins to thicken. Set
aside. Cut the cheeses in half horizontally and top each of them with a thick smear of
the rosemary cream. Place on a plate and refrigerate until needed.

For the relish, place the onion, vinegar, and sugar in a small pan and cook gently
for 6–8 minutes to form a light syrup. Add the chopped apricots, their juices, and the
raisins and cook for 5–8 minutes or until the apricots become thick and jam-like in
consistency. Remove and keep warm.

For the pistachio oil, place the pistachios and oil in a blender and blend for about
1 minute until smooth. Remove and strain through a muslin cloth (ideally) or a
fine strainer.

Toast the thin roll slices under the broiler on both sides, then brush them liberally
with olive oil. Place the cheeses on a broiler pan and place under the broiler, as close
as you can bear to the heat itself, until they are golden and glazed beautifully. Place
1 spoonful of relish on each toasted roll slice and top with a slice of chèvre. Garnish
the cheeses with some buckler leaf sorrel or watercress and a drizzle of pistachio oil.

Vine-baked camembert
with pepper-cranberry jelly and fennel salsa

Putting these vine leaves in the oven imparts an almost lemony taste to
the cheese, while the peppercorns add a pleasant kick. Serve with plenty
of toasted country bread.

for the pepper-cranberry jelly

8-ounce jar cranberry jelly

*1 teaspoon green peppercorns in brine, drained and
    lightly crushed*

1 teaspoon vege-gel (vegetarian alternative to gelatin)

1 camembert cheese, cut into 6 equal wedges

1/2 teaspoon olive oil

1/2 teaspoon coarsely cracked black pepper

12 vine leaves in brine, drained

for the fennel salsa

4 tablespoons extra-virgin olive oil

1 head fennel, trimmed and cut into 1/2 inch dice

1 garlic clove, crushed

1 tablespoon balsamic vinegar

2 teaspoons unsalted butter

juice of 1/2 lemon

2 green onions, chopped

1 tablespoon chopped fresh cilantro

4 sun-dried tomatoes in oil, drained and chopped

salt and freshly ground black pepper

serves 6

For the jelly, melt the cranberry jelly in a pan over a moderate heat. Stir in the
crushed green peppercorns and cook for 1 minute. Sprinkle over the vege-gel, stir in
and heat until the jelly thickens. Pour into a small bowl and refrigerate overnight or
until set.

Preheat the oven to 375°F. Brush the camembert wedges with a little olive oil
and a little seasoning of black pepper.

Rinse the vine leaves under cold running water, then dry them in a dry cloth.
Place two overlapping vine leaves on a flat surface, then set one wedge of cheese in
the center of the overlapping vine leaves and bring up the sides to neatly wrap the
cheese. Prepare the remaining five wedges in the same manner. Place the wrapped
cheeses on a large cookie sheet and set aside.

For the fennel salsa, heat half the oil in a pan over a moderate heat, add the
fennel, and cook for 3–4 minutes until softened. Transfer to a bowl, add the
remaining ingredients, and season to taste. Leave to cool.

Place the cheeses in the oven for 4–5 minutes. Place a baked camembert on
each serving plate, garnish with a good spoon of jelly, and pour around some of the
fennel salsa. Serve immediately.

Marinated oyster mushrooms
with basil and ginger

You can use shiitake or chestnut mushrooms instead. Don't chill before
serving because the delicate marinating juices dilute the flavor.

¹/3 inch piece of fresh ginger, peeled and chopped

2 garlic cloves, peeled and thinly sliced

2 green chilies, deseeded and thinly sliced

1 pound oyster mushrooms

2 tablespoons peanut or vegetable oil

2 tablespoons light soy sauce

1 teaspoon palm sugar or brown sugar

1 tablespoon fresh lemon juice

1 ounce thai basil (or sweet basil)

coarse sea salt and freshly ground black pepper

Place the chopped ginger, garlic, and chili in a mortar, add a little salt and crush lightly with the pestle to form a smooth paste. Trim the oyster mushrooms and clean them of any dirt with a damp cloth, then cut them into bite-size pieces if necessary.

Heat the oil in a wok or large skillet and, when hot, add the paste and cook for 20–30 seconds to infuse the oil. Throw in the mushrooms and cook for 3–4 minutes. Add the soy sauce and sugar and cook for a further 1 minute. Adjust the seasoning, add the lemon juice and basil, toss together, and remove from the heat. Transfer to a bowl and leave to cool before serving at room temperature.

Chinese-fried asparagus
with miso and sesame

An oriental way of enjoying asparagus that takes only minutes to make.

1 tablespoon sesame seeds

2 tablespoons vegetable or sunflower oil

1 inch piece of fresh ginger, peeled and grated

1 garlic clove, crushed

1 teaspoon white miso

2 tablespoons mirin

24 asparagus, peeled, trimmed and cut into 2 inch pieces

1 teaspoon sugar

cracked black pepper

2 teaspoons sesame oil

2 tablespoons soy sauce

Heat a large skillet or wok, add the sesame seeds and dry-fry over a high heat for 1 minute or until golden. Set aside. Return the pan to the heat, add the oil, ginger, garlic, miso, and mirin and mix well. Add the asparagus and stir-fry for 2–3 minutes or until almost tender. Sprinkle over the sugar and a little cracked black pepper and stir-fry for a further 1 minute.

Divide among four serving plates and spoon over the sesame oil, soy sauce, and sesame seeds. Serve immediately.

Spanish romescu baby leeks

A simple dish using leeks poached in an aromatic broth, lifted with a
purée of red bell peppers, chili, and almonds. It is ideally eaten at room
temperature to appreciate it at its best. Artichokes are also good served
this way. Serve with lots of crusty bread to mop up the wonderful juices.

for the purée

4 tablespoons extra-virgin olive oil

1 slice of country-style loaf, crusts removed

juice of 1/4 lemon

2 garlic cloves, crushed

3/4 cup almonds, peeled and toasted

2 red bell peppers, roasted and peeled

1 teaspoon tomato paste

1 red chili

1/2 pound ripe tomatoes

4 tablespoons extra-virgin olive oil

1 tablespoon dry white wine

1/2 teaspoon sugar

1 bay leaf

sprig of thyme

sprig of rosemary

1 garlic clove, crushed

4 coriander seeds, crushed

1 pound baby leeks, trimmed, but left whole

1 tablespoon chopped fresh flat-leaf parsley

salt and freshly ground black pepper

For the purée, heat the olive oil in a skillet over a moderate heat, add the bread, and
fry until golden. Transfer to a food processor and add the lemon juice, garlic, and
almonds and blend to a smooth paste. Add the roasted peppers, tomato purée, chili,
and tomatoes and blend again until smooth and creamy in texture.

Place the oil, wine, sugar, bay leaf, thyme, rosemary, garlic, and coriander seeds
and 2 1/2 cups water in a pan, bring to a boil, and simmer for 10 minutes. Add the
leeks and simmer for 15–20 minutes or until the leeks are tender. Remove the leeks
and place them in a dish. Remove the bay leaf, thyme, and rosemary from the
cooking liquid. Add the purée to the cooking liquid, whisk well together, and season
to taste.

Place the leeks on a serving dish, pour the romescu broth over the leeks, and
leave to cool. Serve at room temperature or cold, garnished with the chopped parsley.

Stuffed riesling-braised artichokes
with herb-infused oil

Serving fresh artichokes is always an impressive affair, but they do need a lot of preparation which is, I feel, the reason why they are not as popular to cook at home as they should be. They can be prepared up to the filling stage well in advance, then finished when needed.

4 globe artichokes, about 10 ounces each

2 lemons, halved

4 tablespoons olive oil

1 small onion, finely chopped

1 garlic clove, crushed

$^1/_4$ pound wild (or cultivated) mushrooms, coarsely chopped

5 ounces fresh spinach

4 tablespoons heavy cream

3 tablespoons chopped walnuts

$^1/_4$ cup freshly grated castelli vegetalia (parmesan-style cheese)

$^1/_2$ cup fresh breadcrumbs

$^1/_2$ cup Riesling wine or other dry white wine

large sprig of lemon thyme (or thyme)

$2^1/_2$ tablespoons unsalted butter

$^1/_2$ teaspoon lemon zest

3 tablespoons fresh herbs (tarragon, chervil, chives, flat-leaf parsley)

salt and freshly ground black pepper

Preheat the oven to 350°F. Using a large sharp knife, trim about 2 inches from the top of each artichoke and, using kitchen scissors, cut off the thorny top third of the leaves. Squeeze the lemons into a large pot of lightly salted boiling water, add the artichokes, and top with a plate which will keep the artichokes submerged in the water as they cook. Cook for 18–20 minutes or until the outer leaves of the artichokes can be pulled out easily. Remove the artichokes with a slotted spoon, let them drain, and cool upside down on a dish towel. Retain the cooking liquid.

To prepare the stuffing, heat 3 tablespoons of the oil in a frying pan, add the onion, garlic, and mushrooms, and cook over a moderate heat for 2–3 minutes until softened. Add the spinach and cook until all the water has evaporated. Add the cream and walnuts and cook for a further 2 minutes. Place in a food processor and blend until smooth. Add the castelli vegetalia and breadcrumbs and mix well to bind. Transfer back to the pan and cook for 1 minute. Season to taste and remove to a bowl to cool.

Remove the tiny hairy chokes from each artichoke with a teaspoon. Fill the center of each artichoke with the stuffing, pressing it down well into the base. Place the stuffed artichokes in a suitable size casserole dish, pour over the white wine, the remaining olive oil and $1^1/_4$ cups reserved artichoke cooking liquid, tuck in the lemon thyme and place in the oven to bake for 15–20 minutes.

Place the artichokes in four individual shallow bowls or soup plates. Strain the cooking liquid into a small pan, bring to a boil, and then simmer until reduced in volume. Whisk in the butter, lemon zest, and herbs, season to taste, and pour around the artichokes to serve.

Cheese and tomato French toasts
with green bean and shallot vinaigrette

A savory French toast appetizer idea; the same principle could apply to many other delicious fillings on the same lines, such as chèvre and olives. Always choose the best quality bread you can for these French toasts.

1/2 stick unsalted butter, softened

8 slices of thin white bread

5 ounces vegetarian Swiss cheese, thinly sliced

2 tablespoons good quality pesto sauce (bought or home-made—see PG TIPS page 103)

1/2 cup semidry tomatoes, drained, oil reserved

1/2 cup light cream

1 large free-range egg

2 tablespoons finely grated castelli vegetalia (parmesan-style cheese)

little clarified butter (see PG TIPS page 171) or olive oil

salt, freshly ground black pepper and ground nutmeg

for the bean and shallot vinaigrette

7 ounces cooked French string beans

2 shallots, finely chopped

6 black olives, stoned and finely chopped

1/2 garlic clove, crushed

1 red chili, deseeded and finely chopped

4 tablespoons reserved oil from sunblush tomatoes

juice of 1/2 lemon

salt and freshly ground black pepper

Spread the butter on both sides of each bread slice, top four of the slices with Swiss cheese, and layer over the pesto. Scatter some semidry tomatoes over the pesto, then close up the sandwiches with the remaining slices of buttered bread, pressing down firmly to make them compact. Cut out each sandwich into circles using a 2/3 inch diameter cutter.

In a shallow tray, whisk together the cream, egg, and castelli vegetalia; add a little seasoning of salt, pepper, and nutmeg. Heat a large nonstick skillet with the clarified butter or oil and when it's fairly hot immerse the sandwiches in the cream mixture, shaking off any excess, and place into the pan. Cook over a moderate heat for 2 minutes on each side until golden in color.

Meanwhile, for the vinaigrette, place the French string beans and chopped shallots in a bowl, add the remaining ingredients, toss well together, and season to taste. Place the salad on four serving plates, top with the French toasts, and serve immediately.

PG TIPS Vegetarian Swiss cheese is available from leading stores. You can also use vegetarian gouda, but it is not so easily accessible.

Raw and cooked porcini mushrooms
with garlic truffle cream and cheese cracknel

A lovely contrast of raw and cooked porcini mushrooms—the king of the mushroom kingdom. They are served with a delicately infused garlic and truffle cream, and feather-light cheese wafers, which are fantastic served with all manner of dishes especially risotto, pasta, and salads.

for the cheese cracknel

1 tablespoon flour

3/4 cup freshly grated castelli vegetalia (parmesan-style cheese)

1 teaspoon unsalted butter, softened

for the garlic truffle cream

4 garlic cloves

1/2 cup milk

5 tablespoons heavy cream

1 teaspoon white truffle oil

4 teaspoons finely grated castelli vegetalia (parmesan-style cheese)

salt and freshly ground black pepper

1 pound fresh porcini mushrooms, cleaned

1 small garlic clove, crushed

1 teaspoon fresh thyme leaves

1/2 cup extra-virgin olive oil

zest and juice of 1/2 lemon

1/4 pound arugula leaves

salt and freshly ground black pepper

For the cheese cracknel, place the flour and castelli vegetalia in a small bowl and gently rub together with your fingers. Heat a small nonstick skillet over a moderate heat and add the butter. Sprinkle a heaped tablespoon into the pan, press down with a fork into a thin round layer, and leave to cook for 15–20 seconds until the cheese bubbles. Remove with a palette knife and place to one side to cool. Prepare all the mix in the same way.

For the cream, place the garlic and milk in a small pan and gently cook for 15 minutes until the garlic is very soft. Add the cream and transfer to a small food processor and blend until smooth. Place in a bowl and leave to cool. Add the truffle oil, castelli vegetalia, and season to taste.

Divide the mushrooms equally and, with a sharp knife, cut approximately 1/2–1 inch off the base of each stem. Cut half the mushrooms into 1/2 inch thick slices and the other into 1/4 inch slices. Place the thicker slices into a bowl, add a little salt, the garlic, thyme, and half the olive oil. Toss carefully together and set aside. Heat a ridged skillet over a high heat and, when smoking, carefully place the mushroom slices on the skillet and cook for 2–3 minutes, turning them carefully, until golden and caramelized.

Meanwhile place the smaller mushroom slices in another bowl, pour over the remaining olive oil, lemon zest, and juice and season well.

Quickly arrange the grilled and raw mushrooms on four serving plates, toss the arugula leaves with the garlic truffle cream and place in the center of each plate. Garnish the salad with some crispy cheese cracknel and serve immediately.

Avocado salsa rolls
with hot limes

In this recipe all the ingredients of the well loved guacamole come into play, plus a few others using Chef's poetic license. These little rolls not only look wonderful but are packed with great Mexican flavors.

^{1}/2 cup dried black beans (turtle beans)

1 small red onion, finely chopped

4 plum tomatoes, chopped

1^1/2 cups corn (canned are fine)

1 mango, peeled and chopped

3 tablespoons chopped fresh cilantro

4 firm but ripe avocados (preferably Fuerte variety)

few small arugula leaves

for the dressing

1 garlic clove, crushed

1 small red chili, deseeded and finely chopped

juice of 1 lemon

5 tablespoons olive oil

pinch of ground cumin

1 tablespoon maple syrup

2 limes, halved

Soak the black beans in cold water overnight, rinse under cold water and drain. Place them in a pan, cover with water, and bring to a boil. Reduce the heat, simmer for 1^1/2 hours or until tender. Drain and leave to cool thoroughly.

Chop the beans coarsely, then place in a bowl with the onion, tomatoes, corn, mango, and cilantro and toss well to combine.

For the dressing, place all the ingredients in a bowl except for the limes, pour over the bean salad, and leave for 1 hour.

Cut the avocados in half lengthwise and remove the pits. Peel them into long thin slices using a wide-bladed, swivel-headed peeler. Work quickly as they will go brown if left too long exposed to the air. You will need twenty slices in total. Chop any remaining avocado and add to the bean salad. Lay out the avocado slices on a flat surface, fill each with the salad mix, and roll up tightly into neat rolls. Preheat a broiler to its highest setting. Place the lime halves under the broiler for 3–4 minutes until hot (this makes it easier to squeeze out the juice). Place five rolls per serving on a plate and garnish with arugula leaves. Squeeze the limes over the little rolls and serve immediately.

Eggplant kibbeh
with vegetable vinaigrette

Bulgur wheat has a distinctive nutty flavor, due to the inner layers of bran, which marries well with eggplant.

150ml olive oil

1 eggplant, cut into $^1/_3$ inch dice

1 onion, finely chopped

1 garlic clove, crushed

1 teaspoon smoked paprika

$^1/_2$ teaspoon ground cumin

$^1/_2$ cup bulgur (cracked wheat), cooked

juice of 1 lemon

1 beef tomato, blanched, peeled, and quartered

fresh cilantro leaves

salt and freshly ground black pepper

for the vegetable vinaigrette

$^1/_2$ roasted red bell pepper, peeled and diced

$^1/_2$ roasted green bell pepper, peeled and diced

2 teaspoons superfine capers

1 tablespoon chopped fresh cilantro

3 tablespoons chopped fresh mint

2 tablespoons sherry vinegar

6 tablespoons olive oil

pinch of sugar

salt and freshly ground black pepper

for the mint yogurt

4 tablespoons natural yogurt

1 tablespoon chopped fresh mint

For the kibbeh, heat $^1/_2$ cup olive oil in a skillet over a moderate heat. Add the eggplant and fry until golden. Add the onion, garlic, paprika, and cumin and cook for a further 5–8 minutes. Add the cooked bulgur and sauté together for 2 minutes. Season to taste and leave to cool. Add the lemon juice and remaining oil.

For the vinaigrette, mix all the ingredients together in a bowl and season to taste. For the mint yogurt, mix the yogurt and mint together in a bowl.

Take a 2 inch cutter and place on a serving plate. Fill with the kibbeh mixture. Using another 2 inch cutter, cut out a circle from each quarter of tomato and place on the kibbeh and press down to compress the mixture. Prepare four servings in the same way and brush the tops with olive oil. Spoon the vinaigrette around each kibbeh and garnish with a spoonful of the mint yogurt. Serve chilled and garnish with cilantro leaves.

Eggplant and tomato rolls
with whipped pomegranate and chili yogurt

This is my up-scale version of baba ghanoush, infused heartily with lots of bright fresh herbs and spices. Some flatbread makes a great accompaniment.

2 large eggplants

6 tablespoons olive oil

1 lemon, halved

4 garlic cloves, unpeeled

2 large green chilies, chopped

3 tablespoons fresh mint leaves

6 tablespoons fresh coriander leaves

1 teaspoon cumin seeds, dry-roasted

1 teaspoon cardamom seeds, dry-roasted

4 beef tomatoes, firm but juicy and ripe

eggplant chips (see PG TIPS)—optional

8 lemon wedges

salt and freshly ground black pepper

for the pomegranate and chili yogurt

1 teaspoon chili oil

$^1/4$ cup thick natural yogurt

2 green onions, finely chopped

$^1/2$ garlic clove, crushed

1 fresh pomegranate, halved and seeds squeezed out

1 tablespoon chopped fresh mint

salt and freshly ground black pepper

Preheat the oven to 450°F. Place the eggplants on a foil lined cookie sheet, prick them all over with a sharp knife, and drizzle with 5 tablespoons of olive oil. Place the lemon halves and garlic cloves alongside, put in the oven, and roast for 25–30 minutes until the eggplants are very tender and charred all over. Remove and cool.

Place the green chilies, mint, cilantro, dry-roasted spices, and the remaining olive oil into a food processor and blend to a paste.

Halve the eggplants and carefully scoop out the inner flesh, leaving the skin. Place in a colander or muslin cloth and squeeze out the excess moisture. Add the flesh with the peeled roasted garlic to the spices in the food processor and blend to a smooth thick purée, scraping down the sides if necessary. Remove to a bowl, add the juices from the roasted lemon halves, and season well to taste. Refrigerate until needed.

Using a kitchen mandolin or very sharp thin-bladed knife, cut the tomatoes into very thin slices. For each roll, lay out three rows of three overlapping slices of tomatoes on a small piece of plastic wrap. Spoon on the chilled eggplant mixture and use the plastic wrap to lift and roll each into a pancake with twisted ends. Gently seal into a bonbon shape, then refrigerate for 30 minutes.

Meanwhile, fry the eggplant chips (if using). For the pomegranate and chili yogurt, whip the chili oil and yogurt together, add the green onions, garlic, pomegranate seeds, and mint, and season to taste.

Carefully unroll the plastic wrap from the tomato rolls and gently place one on each serving plate, garnish with the eggplant chips, lemon wedges, and a good dollop of the yogurt. Serve immediately.

PG TIPS For the eggplant chips, thinly slice 1 eggplant into $^1/8$ inch thick slices, using a kitchen mandolin or thin-bladed knife. Lay on a tray and lightly season with salt to extract the excess water and leave for 30 minutes. Rinse lightly and dry well. Deep-fry them in hot vegetable oil at 325°F until golden and crisp. Remove onto paper towels to drain off any excess fat and keep at room temperature until ready for use.

Tuscan tomato bread pudding
with peas and fava beans

These individual little savory bread puddings are delicious on their own, but paired with the delicate tasting spring peas and beans, bound in a little sauce made from their natural juices, takes them straight to heaven! Store-bought semidry tomatoes may be used instead of your own oven-dried tomatoes if you wish.

¹/2 cup full-fat milk

³/4 cup heavy cream

2 sprigs of fresh rosemary

2 free-range eggs

1 free-range egg yolk

2 ounces ricotta cheese

2 crusty bread rolls, cut into 1cm slices

1 tablespoon extra-virgin olive oil

4 slices of mild chèvre

¹/2 cup oven-dried tomatoes (see PG TIPS), chopped

2 tablespoons pesto sauce (see PG TIPS page 103)

salt, freshly ground black pepper and ground nutmeg

for the vegetables

2 cups fresh fava beans, shelled

1 cup fresh peas, shelled

¹/2 cup good vegetable broth

3 tablespoons fresh tarragon leaves, chopped

1 shallot, finely chopped

1 tablespoon unsalted butter, chilled and diced

2 tablespoons extra-virgin olive oil

4 x ¹/2 cup ramekins

Preheat the oven to 350°F. Place the milk, cream, and rosemary in a small pan, bring to a boil, and simmer for 2–3 minutes. Remove from the heat, leave unstrained to infuse and cool. Strain through a fine strainer.

In a bowl, whisk together the eggs and egg yolk and gradually pour into the cream; season to taste with salt, pepper, and nutmeg. Add the ricotta and mix well.

Butter four ramekins and place them in a roasting tin. Brush the bread slices with olive oil and arrange in the bases of the ramekins. Place the slices of chèvre on top and scatter over the oven-dried tomatoes. Gently pour over the prepared cream and fill to the top. Don't worry if the bread floats to the surface. Place the ramekins in a roasting pan and pour boiling water in the pan so it reaches halfway up the sides of the ramekins. Place in the oven for 30–40 minutes until cooked, then remove the dishes from the roasting pan. Keep them warm while you prepare the vegetables.

Blanch the fava beans in boiling water for 2 minutes, remove with a slotted spoon into iced water, and then peel them. Cook the peas for 2–3 minutes and drain well. Heat the vegetable broth with 2 tablespoons chopped tarragon and the shallot and leave to simmer for 1 minute. Place half the fava beans in a food processor with the tarragon broth and blend to a smooth creamy purée. Place the purée in a pan with the remaining beans and cooked peas and warm over a low heat. Add the butter, a little at a time, season to taste, and add the remaining chopped tarragon and olive oil.

Turn out the tomato puddings onto serving plates, drizzle a little of the pesto over each bread topping. Spoon the peas and beans around the puddings and garnish with a sprig of rosemary, if desired. Serve immediately.

PG TIPS For the oven-dried tomatoes, take 2 pounds blanched, peeled, and deseeded plum tomatoes, then halve them lengthwise. Arrange the tomatoes side by side on a baking dish, sprinkle lightly with sea salt and sugar, then scatter over some fresh thyme leaves. Drizzle with olive oil, place in a preheated oven, set at its lowest setting. Cook for about 1 hour, until very soft, then turn the tomatoes over, baste with their juices and cook for a further 1 hour, by which time they should be tender and shriveled to half the size. Cover with a little olive oil and refrigerate until needed.

Vegetable carpaccio
with saffron verde dressing—RAW

A vibrant and tasty raw vegetable appetizer from Piedmont in Italy. Its success is reliant on the superb quality of the raw vegetables used, sliced as thinly as possible and prepared just before serving.

for the dressing

1 garlic clove, crushed

6 tablespoons fresh flat-leaf parsley

1/2 teaspoon red chili, finely chopped

1/2 cup extra-virgin olive oil

1/2 teaspoon powdered saffron

1/2 teaspoon Dijon mustard

1/3 cup fresh white breadcrumbs

1 teaspoon balsamic vinegar

1 tablespoon white wine vinegar

salt and freshly ground black pepper

2 small beets, trimmed and peeled

1 large head of fennel, peeled

2 stalks of celery, peeled

1 small cauliflower, florets only

4 red radishes

1 large zucchini

1 small avocado, halved and pitted

For the dressing, place the garlic, parsley, chili, and oil in a blender or food processor and blend to a coarse pulp. Add the saffron and mustard. Soak the breadcrumbs with the vinegars for 1 minute, then add to the oil. Blend again briefly and season to taste.

Using a sharp knife or, better still, a kitchen mandolin, slice all the vegetables into thin shavings. Cut the avocado into thin slices. Arrange the vegetables attractively, with an eye for color, on four serving plates, drizzle over the dressing, and serve with lots of country-style bread.

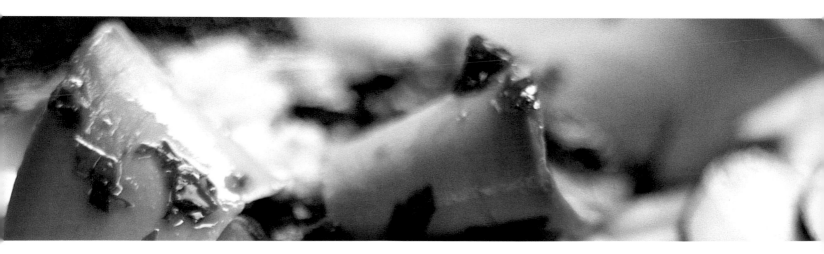

Beet caponata

One of the greatest dishes for me in the Italian repertoire is caponata, a type of sweet and sour relish. It's best made up to two days in advance to allow the flavors to develop. Traditionally made with eggplant and celery, my variation uses roast beet delicately flavored with fresh basil and mint. This dish is great served with lots of crusty bread; sometimes I like to top it with grilled chèvre.

2 large raw beets

4 tablespoons extra-virgin olive oil

1 red onion, chopped

2 stalks of celery, stringed, cut into $^1/_3$ inch dice

2 tablespoons raisins

12 green olives, pitted

2 tablespoons superfine capers, rinsed and drained

3 tablespoons red wine vinegar

1 tablespoon balsamic vinegar

2 tablespoons brown sugar

2 tablespoons pine nuts, toasted

1 tablespoon chopped fresh purple basil
   (or green basil)

1 tablespoon chopped fresh mint

Preheat the oven to 350°F. Wash the beets, drizzle with half the olive oil, and wrap them in foil. Place on a cookie sheet and cook in the oven for up to $1^1/_2$ hours or until tender. Remove and cool before carefully peeling off their skins. Cut the beets into $^1/_3$ inch dice.

Heat the remaining oil in a large skillet, add the onion, and cook over a low heat until just softened. Add the celery and raisins and cook for a further 1 minute. Add the beets, olives, and capers and mix well. Pour over the vinegars, add the sugar, and raise the heat. Cook for 5–6 minutes until the syrup around the beets becomes sticky and jam-like in consistency. Add the pine nuts and herbs. Leave to cool to room temperature, then store in the fridge for up to 2 days before serving.

On the day, allow the caponata to come to room temperature before serving.

Baby shallots roasted in marsala
with peppers and basil

Shallots benefit from slow-roasting in an oven—they soften and release their natural sweetness during the process.

2 tablespoons vegetable or sunflower oil

1 pound medium-size shallots, peeled, with root intact

pinch of ground cardamom

salt

1 tablespoon soft brown sugar

2 tablespoons balsamic vinegar

1 cup marsala wine

4 red bell peppers

8 sun-dried tomatoes in oil, chopped

12 small basil leaves

Heat the oven to 400°F. Heat the oil in a roasting pan large enough for the shallots on a burner and sauté them over a moderate heat until golden. Season with the ground cardamom, and salt, and sprinkle over the sugar. Lightly caramelize the shallots for 2–3 minutes, then pour over the vinegar, marsala, and $1/2$ cup water. Bring to a boil, then transfer, uncovered, to the oven. Roast the shallots for 20–25 minutes, shaking the pan from time to time and basting them with the pan juices until they are soft, well colored, and glazed beautifully.

Meanwhile place the peppers in another roasting pan and cook for 20–25 minutes until the skins are blackened. Transfer to a bowl and cover with plastic wrap for 5 minutes to loosen their skins. Skin, halve, and deseed the peppers, then cut into wide strips. Place on four plates, scatter over the tomatoes, and drizzle with some of their preserving oil. Top with the warm shallots, scatter over the basil leaves, and serve.

Zaatar crushed labna
with parsley, mint, and olive oil

Zaatar is a dry spice and seed mixture popular throughout the Middle East. It is composed of dried thyme, sumac (a lemon-tasting red berry that is dried), and sesame seeds. It is purchased in its made-up form.

20 small labna cheese balls, drained and dried

3 tablespoons zaatar spice mix

2 plum tomatoes, cut into small dice

1 shallot, finely chopped

2 tablespoons fresh mint leaves, chopped

2 tablespoons fresh flat-leaf parsley, chopped

$1/2$ cup mild olive oil

Middle Eastern style flatbread

Place the labna balls in a bowl, sprinkle over the zaatar, and toss lightly to ensure an even coating. Set aside for 1 hour. Using a fork, lightly crush the cheese. Add the tomatoes, shallot, and herbs and toss together again. Place on serving plates in a pile, drizzle over the olive oil, and serve with warmed flatbread.

Grilled portobello mushroooms
with mozzarella "en carrozza" and pistachio pesto

If buffalo mozzarella is not available use cow's milk mozzarella. Panko
crumbs are freeze-dried, which means they prevent the oil from soaking
into the crumbs during frying. They can be sourced from oriental stores.
Of course ordinary breadcrumbs could be used.

for the tomato vinaigrette

1/2 cup ripe tomatoes, chopped

2 tablespoons red wine vinegar

2 tablespoons tomato ketchup

1 teaspoon tomato paste

4 tablespoons extra-virgin olive oil

for the pistachio pesto

20 fresh basil leaves

1 ounce pine nuts

1 ounce pistachio nuts

3 garlic cloves, crushed

3/4 cup extra-virgin olive oil

1 tablespoon freshly grated castelli vegetalia
  (parmesan-style cheese)

4 medium portobello mushrooms,

4 tablespoons extra-virgin olive oil

1 teaspoon fresh oregano

4 x 1/3 inch thick slices buffalo mozzarella

plain flour for coating

2 free-range eggs, beaten

3/4 cup Japanese breadcrumbs (panko)

4 beef tomatoes, blanched, peeled and cut into
  1/3 inch thick slices

salt and freshly ground black pepper

For the tomato vinaigrette, place all the ingredients in a small food processor and blend for 30 seconds. Strain through a fine strainer and refrigerate until needed.

For the pesto, put all the ingredients in a blender and blend to a coarse paste. Set aside.

Slice each mushroom cap horizontally. Brush with a little olive oil on both sides of each slice and place on a cookie sheet, cut-side up. Season well.

Sprinkle oregano and a little seasoning over the mozzarella and carefully dredge the pieces in flour, then into beaten egg, and finally through the breadcrumbs.

Heat a ridged skillet, brush with a little olive oil, and fry the mushrooms for 3–4 minutes until golden and lightly charred all over.

Meanwhile heat the remaining oil in a large skillet, add the mozzarella slices and cook for 2–3 minutes on each side until golden. Remove and drain on paper towels. Place four mushroom bases on individual plates, put a well seasoned slice of tomato on top, and then a slice of fried mozzarella. Place the mushroom lids on the top to reform the original shape. Add a good spoonful of the pistachio pesto and drizzle some tomato vinaigrette around the plate to serve.

Soups

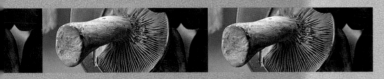

Why is it that soup is so often considered to be an unadventurous and safe option for serving as an appetizer? Of course this is not how soups should be or need be! Soups are one of the most satisfying of foods, whether served chilled in the height of summer or hot to ward off the cold in winter months. The secret of any well prepared soup is the inclusion of an excellent basic broth.

Spelt soup
with Jerusalem artichokes and saffron

Modern cooks are rediscovering the full flavor of whole grains like spelt, and not before time. They have long been popular in Europe, especially Italy, where spelt is more commonly known as *farro* and is used in all manner of tasty dishes. It is very nutritious and the perfect answer for those people who want to eat good, hearty grain products.
It is available from health food stores.

1 cup fine spelt (preferably organic)

1/2 stick unsalted butter

1 onion, chopped

1 garlic clove, crushed

3/4 pound Jerusalem artichokes, well scrubbed and thinly sliced

6 fresh sage leaves

pinch of saffron

3 cups good vegetable broth, hot

5 ounces light cream

3 tablespoons pecorino cheese (ewe's milk cheese)

1 tablespoon extra-virgin olive oil

salt and freshly cracked black pepper

Soak the spelt overnight in a bowl of cold water and drain.

Melt the butter in a pan, add the onion and garlic, and cook for 3–4 minutes until slightly softened. Add the artichokes, sage, and saffron and mix well. Pour in the hot vegetable broth and bring to a boil. Add the spelt, cover, and simmer gently for 20–25 minutes or until the artichokes are tender. (Reserve 2 tablespoons cooked spelt for the garnish.) Transfer to a food processor and blend until smooth, then return the soup to a clean pan. Add the cream and return to a boil; season with salt and freshly cracked black pepper.

Meanwhile, grate the pecorino cheese as fine as possible and mix it with the reserved spelt in a bowl. Divide the soup among four serving bowls, sprinkle over the spelt and pecorino mixture, and drizzle over the olive oil. Serve immediately.

Mushroom Tom Yum

This soup has its origins firmly rooted in the southern Asian region of Thailand. Classic Tom Yum soup contains fish or meat, but this variation using wild mushrooms lacks nothing less than the former. Galangal is a type of camphorized fresh ginger available from Thai stores, although fresh ginger could be used instead. The use of shiitake mushrooms adds a meaty flavor to the broth.

2 pints good vegetable broth

1 1/2 inch piece of galangal, peeled, cut into thin slices

2 stalks of lemongrass, outer casing discarded, thinly shredded

1 tablespoon vegetarian fish sauce (nuoc mam chay)

3 kaffir lime leaves, torn into small pieces

5 ounces wild mushrooms of your choice (including shiitake, or use all shiitake)

2 teaspoons red Thai curry paste

2 large shallots, thinly sliced

3 tomatoes, cut into 1/2 inch dice

juice of 2 limes

little coarse sea salt

3 tablespoons fresh cilantro leaves

Bring the vegetable broth to a boil, add the galangal and lemongrass, and cook for 3–4 minutes. Add the fish sauce, lime leaves, and mushrooms and simmer for 5 minutes. Stir in the curry paste. Add the shallots and diced tomatoes and cook for a further 2 minutes. Finish with the lime juice and a little salt. Taste the soup—it should be spicy, sour, and a little salty. Pour into individual soup bowls and scatter over the cilantro leaves.

Spiced carrot soup

with crispy egg noodles and Vietnamese mint

In this Asian soup (Tom Kha), coconut milk adds a wonderful sweet creaminess, while the mint adds a refreshing fragrance. Egg noodles can be purchased from leading stores or oriental grocers. Vietnamese mint or "hot" mint is in fact not a mint at all. Revered in the Far East, it has a slightly spicy, acidic flavor. It's worth shopping around for but normal mint is fine if it's not available.

vegetable oil for deep-frying

3 1/2 ounces egg noodles

2 tablespoons unsalted butter

2 garlic cloves, crushed

1 teaspoon Thai yellow curry paste

1 pound carrots, peeled and cut into 1/2 inch dice

1 onion, chopped

2 stalks of lemongrass, outer casing discarded,
  finely shredded

3/4 inch piece of fresh ginger, peeled and thinly shredded

3 cups good vegetable broth

juice of 1/2 lime

10 leaves Vietnamese mint, torn

3/4 cup coconut milk

2 green onions, finely chopped

8 lime wedges

Heat the vegetable oil in a large pan or fryer. When the temperature is about 325°F, add the noodles and fry for about 1 minute until crisp. Remove with a slotted spoon and drain on paper towels. Set aside.

Heat the butter in a pan, add the garlic and curry paste, and cook together for 30 seconds. Add the diced carrot, onion, lemongrass, and ginger and cook for 2–3 minutes. Pour in the vegetable broth, add the lime juice, and bring to a boil. Reduce the heat and simmer for 10–15 minutes. Add the mint and coconut milk and cook for a further 1 minute.

Serve in individual soup bowls and top with a small nest of the crispy egg noodles. Scatter over the green onions and serve with the lime wedges for your guests to squeeze over the soup.

Cajun black bean soup

with smoked tomato nachos

For a chunkier version of this soup, leave the beans whole. To quick-soak the beans, cover them in cold water, bring to a boil, and cook, uncovered, over a moderate heat for 2 minutes. Leave to soak, covered, for 1 hour.

1/2 teaspoon black peppercorns

1/2 teaspoon coriander seeds

1/2 teaspoon cumin seeds

1 small bay leaf

1/2 teaspoon cayenne pepper

2 tablespoons fresh oregano, chopped

2 teaspoons fresh thyme, picked

1/2 stick unsalted butter

1 onion, chopped

1 stalk of celery, chopped

2 garlic cloves, crushed

2 cups drained black beans, soaked overnight

juice of 1/2 lemon

salt

for the nachos

2 tablespoons olive oil

1 shallot, finely chopped

1 small garlic clove, crushed

1/2 teaspoon smoked paprika

2 cups semidry tomatoes

1 tablespoon chopped fresh cilantro leaves

2 corn tortillas, each cut into 8 wedges

vegetable oil for deep-frying

3 tablespoons grated vegetarian cheddar cheese

little sour cream (optional)

salt and freshly ground black pepper

Grind the peppercorns, seeds, and bay leaf in a mortar or spice grinder, add the cayenne, oregano, and thyme and mix well. Heat the butter in a medium-size pan, add the onion, celery, and garlic and cook for 2–3 minutes. Add the ground spices and cook for a further 3–4 minutes. Add the soaked beans and 6 cups water and bring to a boil. Reduce the heat and simmer for 1 1/2–2 hours or until the beans are tender. Transfer to a food processor and blend until smooth. Adjust the seasoning and add the lemon juice. Set aside.

For the nachos, heat the olive oil in a pan, add the shallot, garlic, smoked paprika, and semidry tomatoes and cook for 4–5 minutes until softened. Add the chopped cilantro and season to taste. Deep-fry the tortilla wedges until crisp in hot oil and then drain on paper towels. Top with the tomato mixture and sprinkle over the grated cheese. Place the tortillas under a hot preheated broiler until the cheese melts. Meanwhile reheat the soup and then pour into serving bowls and top with 1–2 tomato nachos. Serve with sour cream, if desired.

Fennel soup
with star anise, hazelnuts, and tarragon

This soup is very elegant; in the summer months it is delicious served cold.

$^1/_2$ stick unsalted butter

1 onion, thinly sliced

2 heads of fennel, fronds removed and reserved, thinly sliced

$^1/_2$ pound potatoes, cut into small pieces

$2^1/_2$ cups milk

2 ounces hazelnuts, crushed

3 star anise

$^1/_2$ cup heavy cream

2 tablespoons chopped fresh tarragon

1 tablespoon anise liquor (e.g. Pernod or Ricard)

salt and freshly ground black pepper

Heat the butter in a pan, add the onion and fennel, and cook for about 12–15 minutes, until softened. Add the potatoes, milk, $2^1/_2$ cups water, and hazelnuts and bring to a boil. Add the star anise and simmer for 25 minutes or until all the vegetables are very soft. Remove the star anise and transfer the mixture to a food processor. Blend until very smooth. Return to a clean pan, add the cream, chopped tarragon, and anise liquor, and return to a boil.

Blitz with a handheld blender until light and frothy and season to taste. Pour into serving bowls, scatter over the reserved fennel fronds, and serve.

English pea and mint soup
with truffle ricotta foam

By quickly cooking the vegetables, they retain their color and natural taste.

$3^1/_2$ cups fresh or frozen peas

1 tablespoon fresh mint leaves

1 onion, chopped

1 leek, chopped

3 cups good vegetable broth

1 cup skimmed milk

1 tablespoon extra-virgin olive oil

1 tablespoon unsalted butter

1 teaspoon truffle oil

1 tablespoon unsalted butter

2 tablespoons ricotta cheese

salt and freshly cracked black pepper

Bring a large pan of boiling salted water to a boil. Add the peas, mint leaves, onion, and leek and simmer gently for about 5–6 minutes until tender. Drain them in a colander, then refresh under cold running water. When they are fully drained, transfer to a food processor and blend to a smooth purée, scraping down the sides once or twice to ensure all the purée is satiny smooth.

Place the vegetable broth and $^1/_2$ cup milk in a pan, add the purée, olive oil and butter and bring to a boil, whisking frequently. Season with salt and freshly cracked black pepper.

In another pan, bring the remaining $^1/_2$ cup milk, truffle oil, and butter to a boil. Add the ricotta and blend with a handheld blender until smooth and frothy. Divide the soup among four bowls, then spoon over the ricotta foam to serve.

Fruit ceviche soup
with Thai basil oil—RAW

This welcoming summer soup is an adaptation of one of my old recipes,
but in this version the fruits take on more definition and texture, while
the drizzle of Thai basil oil adds that magical taste of fragrant aniseed.

for the oil
3 tablespoons Thai basil (holy basil)

5 tablespoons groundnut or vegetable oil

for the soup
1¹/2 cups fresh pineapple, diced

1 ripe mango, diced

¹/2 inch piece of fresh ginger, peeled and finely grated

1 tablespoon tamarind paste

2 tablespoons maple syrup

1¹/4 cups fresh orange juice

freshly cracked black pepper

for the fruit ceviche
²/3 cup fresh pineapple, cut into ¹/4 inch dice

¹/2 mango, cut into ¹/4 inch dice

small wedge of orange

fresh melon (charentais or cantaloupe) cut into 5mm dice

1 small red onion, finely chopped

2 kiwis, cut into ¹/4 inch dice

1 pasilla chili, deseeded, finely chopped

juice of 2 limes, zest of 1

For the oil, place the basil and oil in a blender and blend to a purée, then strain it and refrigerate, covered, until needed.

For the soup, place the pineapple, mango, and ginger in a bowl and leave to marinate at room temperature for 1 hour.

Meanwhile for the ceviche, place all the ingredients in a bowl and toss well together. Set aside.

Place the marinated fruits and ginger in a food processor and add the tamarind paste, maple syrup, and orange juice. Blend to a fine purée and then strain or sieve into a bowl. Chill for a good 2–3 hours.

Place the ceviche into the center of four well-chilled shallow soup bowls, pour over the soup, crack over some fresh black pepper, and drizzle Thai basil oil over. Serve immediately.

Cool cucumber soup
with Indian spices

Another great summer soup. Being a lover of all foods from the Far East,
this soup makes a regular appearance on my menus. It is light and
delicately spiced and really gets the gastric juices going. If you are serving
the naan bread, I recommend it served hot—it makes a good contrast.

for the curry paste

2 tablespoons mild curry powder

1 tablespoon garam masala

$1/2$ teaspoon mustard seeds

1 teaspoon cumin seeds

2 teaspoons prepared curry paste

1 garlic clove, crushed

for the cucumber soup

2 cucumbers, peeled and halved lengthwise

*1 small red chili, halved, seeds removed and
    finely chopped*

3 cups thick natural yogurt

2 tablespoons chopped fresh mint leaves

little lemon juice

salt and freshly ground black pepper

hot naan bread, cut into fingers (optional)

For the curry paste, mix the curry powder and garam masala in a bowl. Add
3 tablespoons of water and mix to a paste. Set aside.

Heat a skillet over a moderate heat, throw in the mustard and cumin seeds, and
dry-fry them for 20–30 seconds until they give off an aromatic fragrance. Add the
curry paste and garlic, reduce the heat to very low, and cook for 1 minute. Remove
and leave to cool.

For the cucumber soup, remove the seeds from the cucumbers and cut them
into chunks. Place them in a food processor, add the chili and curry paste, and
blend to a fairly smooth liquid. Strain through a sieve. Pour into a bowl, whisk in the
yogurt, add the mint and a squeeze of lemon juice to taste; season. Refrigerate
until needed. Serve in four soup bowls with the naan bread, if using.

Potato cream soup
with wild mushroooms and soft-boiled egg

New potatoes and wild mushrooms combine to make a delicate soup.

1/2 stick unsalted butter

1 onion, chopped

1 large leek, sliced

3/4 pound large new potatoes, peeled and halved

3 cups good vegetable broth, hot

1/2 cup whole milk

4 free-range eggs

5 ounces dried wild mushrooms, soaked in warm
   water for 30 minutes

coarse sea salt and freshly cracked black pepper

Heat half the butter in a pan, add the onion and leek, and cook over a low heat for 4–5 minutes until softened. Add the potatoes and cook for a further 1 minute. Pour over the broth, reduce the heat, and simmer for 20 minutes or until the potatoes are soft. Transfer to a food processor, add the milk and remaining butter, and blend until smooth in texture.

Bring a pan of water to a boil, reduce the heat, add the eggs, and simmer for 4 minutes. Remove the eggs with a slotted spoon and immerse into a bowl of cold water before shelling them carefully, keeping them intact. Return the soup to a clean pan, add the soaked wild mushrooms and soaking liquid, cook for 1 minute, and adjust the seasoning to taste. Place a soft-boiled egg into each serving bowl, pour over the hot soup carefully, and sprinkle the egg with seasoning and serve.

Buttermilk corn bisque
with radish and wild garlic

This is a chilled variation of chowder made with buttermilk.

1 tablespoon unsalted butter

1 onion, chopped

1 stalk of celery, chopped

2 garlic cloves, crushed

sprig of fresh thyme

3 ears of corn, kernels detached, cob centers reserved

1 1/2 cups light cream

1/2 cup buttermilk

4 small red radishes

1 small bunch of wild garlic leaves (or chives)

salt, freshly ground black pepper, and a pinch of
   cayenne pepper

Melt the butter in a large pan, add the onion, celery, garlic, and thyme and leave to cook over a low heat for 10–12 minutes until the vegetables are soft. Add 3 cups water to the vegetables with the cob centers. Bring to a boil, reduce the heat, and simmer for 20 minutes over a gentle heat until the liquid becomes flavorful. Remove the cob centers and discard. Add the corn kernels and cream to the liquid and simmer for 10 minutes. Remove half of the kernels for garnishing and leave to cool.

Transfer the cooled soup to a food processor and blend until smooth. Strain it and then refrigerate until needed. To serve, add the buttermilk, season with salt, pepper, and pinch of cayenne and add the reserved kernels to the soup. Pour into four individual soup bowls. Garnish with a little pile of grated or shredded red radish and some shredded wild garlic leaves. Serve well chilled.

Beet gazpacho
with apple and frozen avocado cream

A real treat for a hot summer's day, this chilled beet soup is
delicately lifted with a little horseradish; try it as it will soon become a
summer favorite.

2¹/4 pounds ripe plum tomatoes, cut into small chunks

1 small onion, chopped

1 small green bell pepper, deseeded, cut into small chunks

1 garlic clove, crushed

1 slice of stale bread

5 tablespoons extra-virgin olive oil

3 tablespoons good quality sherry vinegar

1 tablespoon creamed horseradish

2 roasted beets, peeled and chopped (see
   page 46)

1 Granny Smith apple

salt and freshly ground black pepper

frozen avocado cream (see page 78)

Place the tomatoes, onion, pepper, garlic and bread in a food processor and blend to
a fine purée. With the motor running, gently pour in a thin stream of the oil through
the funnel at the top and blend until it thickens and forms an emulsion. Add the
vinegar, horseradish, and beets, then blend again until smooth; season to taste.
(If you prefer a smoother soup, pass it through a fine strainer too.) The flavor should
be slightly sweet and sour—add a little more vinegar if necessary. Chill for 4 hours
or overnight.

Pour the chilled soup into four shallow soup bowls. Peel the apple, remove the
center core, then shred into fine strips using a kitchen mandolin or with a sharp knife.
Place a ball of avocado cream in the center of each soup and sprinkle over the finely
shredded apple.

Puy lentil bouillabaisse
with wilted spinach, fennel, and saffron rouille

The king of lentils—the puy lentil—is best for this earthy rustic-style soup;
they taste wonderful and hold their shape well during cooking.

for the rouille

1 medium-size potato

1 small garlic clove, crushed

1 small red bell pepper, roasted and peeled

1 free-range egg yolk

pinch of good quality saffron (or powdered)

3 tablespoons extra-virgin olive oil

*salt, freshly ground black pepper and pinch of
    cayenne pepper*

2 tablespoons olive oil

1 onion, chopped

2 garlic cloves, crushed

*pinch of good quality saffron (or 1/2 teaspoon
    powdered saffron)*

1 small head of fennel, cut into 1/4 inch dice

1/2 teaspoon fennel seeds

1 cup puy lentils

1/2 teaspoon mild paprika

4 cups good vegetable broth

5 ounces baby spinach leaves

4 slices of country-style bread, cut into 1/3 inch cubes

For the rouille, cook the potato in its skin in a pan of boiling water (or alternatively bake in the oven), remove, and, when cool enough to handle, peel off the skin. Place the garlic and pepper in a blender and blend to a purée. Add the cooked potato, egg yolk, saffron, salt, pepper, and a good pinch of cayenne pepper. With the motor running, gently pour in a thin stream of oil through the funnel at the top, as if making mayonnaise, until it thickens and forms an emulsion.

Heat 1 tablespoon of olive oil in a pan, add the onion, garlic, saffron, fennel, and fennel seeds and cook for 4–5 minutes until tender. Add the puy lentils, mild paprika, and broth and bring to a boil. Cook rapidly for 2–3 minutes, then reduce the heat, and simmer for 30 minutes or until the lentils are just cooked. Stir in the spinach and allow to wilt in the soup.

Toast the bread cubes (or fry them in a little olive oil) and place in four serving bowls. Pour over the soup and drizzle over 1 tablespoon of olive oil. Serve the saffron rouille alongside for the guests to stir into the soup themselves. Serve hot.

Chilled avocado
and almond milk guacomole—RAW

A delightfully simple soup of Mexican origin that needs no cooking for those of you who are raw food enthusiasts. The soup should be made just before serving, but if you do plan to make it and keep it for several hours, lay plastic wrap over the surface of the bowl—this will stop the surface of the soup from discoloring and darkening if stored for longer than 1 hour.

2 ripe but not too ripe avocados, cold (preferably Haas variety)

1 onion, finely chopped

1 garlic clove, crushed

2 green chilies, deseeded and finely chopped

3 tablespoons fresh coriander leaves

2 tomatoes, cut into small pieces

1¹/4 cups almond milk (see PG TIPS)

2–3 tablespoons lime juice

salt and freshly ground black pepper

¹/2 cup sour cream or crème fraîche

¹/2 avocado, cut into cubes

1 teaspoon lime zest

1 tablespoon fresh cilantro leaves

Halve the avocados, remove the pits and scoop out the flesh into a food processor. Add the onion, garlic, chili, cilantro leaves, tomatoes and almond milk and blend for about 1 minute until smooth. Add 1¹/4 cups water and enough lime juice to add balance to the soup and blend again. Season with salt and freshly ground black pepper. (If you prefer a smoother soup, pass it through a fine strainer too.) Place in a bowl and cover with plastic wrap if storing for later. To serve immediately, pour into shallow soup bowls, top with a good dollop of sour cream, the diced avocado, lime zest, and cilantro leaves. Serve well chilled.

PG TIPS   Nut milks used in raw cooking provide richness and sweetness to a dish. To make almond milk, soak 2¹/3 cups almonds in 2¹/2 cups pure still water (purified or bottled) and soak overnight at room temperature. Rinse the almonds under cold water and drain well. Place in a food processor and add 4 cups purified water and blend until as smooth as possible. Strain through a fine strainer or cheesecloth and then refrigerate until needed.

Roasted pepper passata
with basil yogurt and tomato tartare

Roasting the tomatoes and peppers for this soup really adds depth of flavor to the end result. The addition of a basil-flavored yogurt and a fresh-tasting tomato tartare complete a great soup.

for the passata
8 ripe plum tomatoes, halved
2 red bell peppers, halved, deseeded and chopped small
1 onion, quartered
2 garlic cloves, peeled
sprig of fresh thyme
2 tablespoons olive oil
4 cups good vegetable broth, hot
1 tablespoon tomato paste
salt and freshly ground black pepper

for the basil yogurt
3 tablespoons fresh basil leaves
3 tablespoons extra-virgin olive oil
4 tablespoons natural thick set yogurt

for the tomato tartare
2 plum tomatoes, blanched and seeded
1 small garlic clove, crushed
1 tablespoon maple syrup
juice of 1/2 lime
1 tablespoon chopped fresh basil

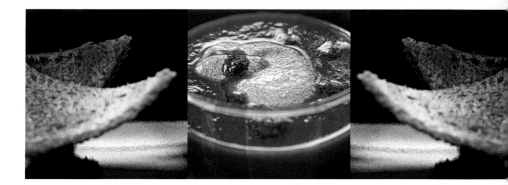

Preheat the oven to 425°F. Place the tomatoes, peppers, onion, garlic, and thyme in a roasting pan, spoon over the olive oil, and season. Roast them for 20–25 mintues, until wilted and slightly charred all over (alternatively, this could be done under a hot broiler). Transfer to a pan, pour over the broth, and add the tomato paste. Cook over a moderate heat for 15 minutes. Strain the soup through a sieve or strainer and return it to a clean pan, adjust the seasoning and keep warm.

For the yogurt, blanch the basil leaves for 15 seconds in boiling water, then remove immediately with a slotted spoon into iced water. Dry the blanched leaves in a cloth. Place the leaves in a small blender with the olive oil and blend until smooth. Break down the yogurt with a small whisk to a creamy texture and stir in the basil oil.

For the tomato tartare, mix all the ingredients in a bowl and season to taste. Reheat the soup to boiling point, then pour into four bowls. Place two good spoonfuls of yogurt in the center of each bowl, followed by a good spoonful of basil on top. Place a little chilled tomato tartare to one side and serve immediately.

PG TIPS A nice accompaniment is crisp melba toasts. Toast slices of white or brown bread under a hot broiler on both sides. Remove the crusts, halve horizontally, and cut into triangles. Grill the untoasted sides for a few seconds until the edges curl. Set aside to cool.

Salads

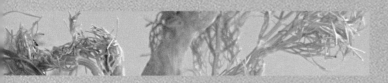

I have always been fascinated by salads—long gone are the days when a simple lettuce mixed with tomato and cucumber sufficed. I have included designer-style salads for the beginner as well as the experienced cook. Vibrant, nutritious, and varied, these salads can be eaten as appetizers, main courses, or for any healthy lunch or supper. I hope they will introduce you to exciting new tastes and combinations from around the globe and act as an inspirational starting point for your own salad creations.

Jerusalem artichoke, bean, and fennel salad
with green peppercorn ajo-blanco

A variation on a salad I recently enjoyed in Alicante in Spain. I've replaced globe artichokes with Jerusalem artichokes and created a peppery almond and garlic dressing to give the salad a pleasant lift. If artichokes are not available, use new potatoes.

for the green peppercorn ajo-blanco
1/2 cup whole blanched almonds

2 tablespoons pine nuts

2 garlic cloves, crushed

1 cup fresh white breadcrumbs

1/2 cup iced water

4 tablespoons extra-virgin olive oil

2 tablespoons sherry vinegar

salt

2 free-range egg yolks

4 tablespoons heavy cream

1 teaspoon green peppercorns, rinsed and drained

16 Jerusalem artichokes

1/2 pound French string beans, topped and tailed

1 large head of fennel, fronds removed

splash of sherry vinegar

2 tablespoons extra-virgin olive oil

1 large shallot, thinly sliced

1/2 cup flaked almonds, toasted

salt and freshly ground black pepper

For the ajo-blanco, place the almonds, pine nuts, and garlic in a food processor and blend them as fine as possible, scraping down the sides of the machine if necessary. Do not overprocess or the nuts will become oily. Add the breadcrumbs and a quarter of the iced water and blend again to a fine purée. With the motor running, gently pour in a thin stream of the oil and half the vinegar through the funnel at the top. When smooth, add the egg yolks and blend again. Strain into a bowl, add salt, and the remaining water and vinegar. Stir in the cream, add the peppercorns and refrigerate until required. Check the consistency before mixing with the vegetables—it should be the consistency of light cream—if it's too thick add a little more water.

Wash and peel the artichokes, cutting off the knobbly bits in order to obtain a cylindrical shape about 1 inch in diameter. Cook them in lightly simmering salted water for 12–15 minutes, according to size. Drain and then slice them into 2 inch thick pieces. Keep warm.

At the same time, cook the French string beans for 5–6 minutes until just tender. Drain well and add to the artichokes.

Using a kitchen mandolin, thinly shave the fennel onto the artichokes and beans, add a splash of vinegar, the olive oil, and shallot slices and season to taste. Add the dressing, toss carefully together, and adjust the seasoning. Place in four salad bowls, garnished with the toasted almonds.

PG TIPS Jerusalem artichokes have a very soft texture when cooked, so it is important to watch them carefully as they cook—the water should not be allowed to boil rapidly or they will become mushy so check their texture regularly as they cook.

Roasted tomato, chèvre, and asparagus salad
with basil purée and lavender oil

Summer is the time to enjoy this most fragrant of salads, made with
perfectly ripe tomatoes, ideally ripened on the vine. The basil purée and
lavender oil completes an air of Provence. I suggest serving this salad
with lots of fresh chunky French bread to mop up the juices.

for the basil purée

1 tablespoon fresh basil leaves (plus some for garnishing)

1 small garlic clove, crushed

6 tablespoons extra-virgin olive oil

for the lavender oil

good sprig of fresh or dried lavender

6 tablespoons extra-virgin olive oil

for the salad

20 small (1 1/2 inch) vine-ripened tomatoes

1 teaspoon superfine sugar

1 teaspoon fresh thyme leaves

*4 mature chèvres (or 2 logs), cut
  to make 20 thin slices*

8 asparagus tips, prepared

12 black olives, stoned

2 tablespoons extra-virgin olive oil

1 tablespoon red wine vinegar

1 tablespoon balsamic vinegar

salt and freshly ground black pepper

Preheat the oven to 350°F. For the basil purée, place the basil and garlic in a blender with the oil and blend to a smooth purée. Transfer to a bowl.

For the lavender oil, remove the flowers from the lavender plant and place in a bowl. Heat the oil in a pan and, when hot, pour in the flowers, remove from the heat and leave to steep for 2 minutes, then strain off the oil. (Leaving to steep any longer tends to make the oil bitter.)

For the salad, remove the tomatoes from their vine, then cut each in half horizontally through the center. Sprinkle the cut tomatoes with salt, pepper, a little sugar and thyme. Place a slice of chèvre between the two halves of each tomato, so that you have twenty reformed tomatoes stuffed with the cheese.

Place the asparagus and olives in a baking dish, pour over the olive oil and roast in the oven for 6–8 minutes. Add the cheese-stuffed tomatoes to the baking dish, drizzle over both vinegars and cook for a further 4–5 minutes or until the tomatoes just begin to soften. Place the baked tomatoes on four serving plates, add the asparagus and olives and drizzle over the basil purée and lavender oil.

Cumin-roasted squash salad

with peppers and chocolate dressing

Don't be put off by the sound of chocolate dressing for the salad. The flavors of the salad are representative of Latino cooking; you will be amazed just how delicate it can be. The combination of spices and chocolate has been used successfully for centuries in South America.

1 large butternut squash, peeled and cut into neat wedges

2 yellow bell peppers, halved and deseeded

1/2 teaspoon cumin seeds

3 tablespoons olive oil

1 red onion, thinly sliced

6 red radishes, thinly sliced

5 tablespoons fresh cilantro leaves

salt and freshly ground black pepper

for the chocolate dressing

1/2 cup fresh orange juice

1/2 garlic clove, crushed

1 tablespoon white wine vinegar

1 tablespoon honey

1/2 teaspoon chili powder

1 tablespoon lime juice

6 tablespoons olive oil

1 ounce good quality bittersweet chocolate (70% cocoa solids), melted and kept warm

salt and freshly ground black pepper

Preheat the oven to 350°F. Place the squash and peppers in a large roasting pan. In a mortar, crush the cumin seeds with a pestle to a fine powder. Season the vegetables with the cumin and drizzle over the olive oil. Place in the oven to roast for 25–30 minutes until tender and slightly caramelized. Remove the peppers from the oven, peel, cut them into thick slices, and return them to the squash. Turn off the oven and keep warm.

For the dressing, place the orange juice in a pan with the garlic, vinegar and honey and bring to a boil. Cook for 2 minutes to form a light syrup. Transfer to a bowl, whisk in the chili powder, lime juice, olive oil, and warm melted chocolate and season to taste. Place the roasted vegetables on four serving plates and scatter over the onion and radish. Pour over the dressing and garnish with the cilantro leaves. Serve warm.

Red tofu salad
with beans, persimmon, mint, and cashews

Although I'm not a great lover of tofu, I can appreciate the enjoyment and
nutritional aspects it can bring. This delicate marinade adds a sweet yet
hot coating to the tofu, topping a wonderfully fragrant and fresh salad.

$^1/_2$ pound firm tofu, drained

2 tablespoons plum sauce

2 tablespoons dark soy sauce

1 tablespoon honey

3 teaspoons sweet chili sauce

2 tablespoons cashew nuts, roasted and roughly chopped

2 persimmons (Sharon fruit), stem removed and cut
 into wedges

$^3/_4$ pound French string beans, topped and tailed

2 tablespoons peanut or vegetable oil

salt and freshly ground black pepper

for the dressing

2 tablespoons palm sugar (or brown sugar)

2 tablespoons coarse sea salt

2 garlic cloves, chopped

good handful of mint leaves

4 hot green chilies, deseeded and chopped

$^1/_3$ inch piece of fresh ginger, peeled and grated

3 tablespoons vegetarian fish sauce (nuoc mam chay)

juice of 8 limes

4 shallots, thinly sliced

Cut the tofu in half widthwise, then cut both pieces in half horizontally to give four
equally thick slices. In a shallow dish combine the plum sauce, soy sauce, honey, and
sweet chili sauce. Place the tofu slices in the marinade and leave to marinate for
2 hours, turning them regularly to make sure the tofu is thoroughly coated. Cook the
beans in a pan of boiling salted water for 2–3 minutes or until just cooked, but still
retaining a good bite.

For the dressing, melt the palm sugar in a small pan. Place the salt, garlic, and
mint in a mortar and lightly pound to a pulp with a pestle. Add the chilies, palm sugar,
and ginger and pound again. Add the fish sauce, lime juice, and shallots and mix well.
Leave for 1 hour for the flavors to develop. Place the cashews, persimmons and
beans in a bowl and pour over the prepared dressing. Toss well and season to taste.
Remove the tofu from the marinade. Heat a large skillet with the oil, add the tofu, and
cook for about 2 minutes on each side until golden and crisp. Place a good pile of
the salad on four serving plates, top each with 1–2 slices of tofu and serve at once.

Grilled baby aubergine salad

with roasted rice and cilantro dressing

Vietnamese cilantro can be found in oriental stores, although regular
cilantro could be substituted.

4 tablespoons sunflower oil

8 baby eggplants

for the dressing

juice of 4 limes, zest of 1

1 tablespoon palm sugar (or brown sugar)

1 small green chili

2 teaspoons kecap manis (Indonesian soy sauce)

2 teaspoons dry-roasted basmati rice (see PG TIPS)

2 banana shallots, peeled and thinly sliced

6 tablespoons fresh Vietnamese cilantro leaves

3 tablespoons fresh mint leaves

salt and freshly ground black pepper

Heat a ridged skillet over a high heat and brush with the oil. Cut the eggplants in half lengthwise, place on the skillet and cook for about 6–8 minutes, turning them regularly, until golden and lightly charred all over.

For the dressing, place the zest and juice of the limes, the palm sugar, chili, and soy sauce in a bowl and stir until the sugar has dissolved. Add the roasted rice, sliced shallots, cilantro, and mint leaves, season to taste, and mix well.

Place the fried eggplants on a large serving platter, spoon over the dressing, and serve immediately.

PG TIPS   To prepare Asian-style roasted rice, heat the oven to 350°F. Place 1 tablespoon basmati rice in a baking tray and put in the oven to dry-roast for 20–25 minutes until golden. Remove and cool. Place in a mortar and crush with the pestle to a coarse powder. Keep in a sealed jar ready for use.

Fava bean crostini salad

with black olive oil and iced chèvre

The new microplane-style graters are fantastic for shaving the iced chèvre at the last minute for this dish. They are now readily available in most good cooking stores. Try to source a mature goat's cheese for this recipe— it will really repay your efforts.

1 firm, mature chèvre

2 ounces pitted black olives

1/2 garlic clove, crushed

1/2 cup extra-virgin olive oil

1 1/2 pounds fresh fava beans, shelled

6 tablespoons young arugula leaves

12 fresh tarragon leaves

1 tablespoon sherry vinegar

1 ciabatta loaf, cut into 8 x 1/3 inch thick slices

salt and freshly ground black pepper

Wrap the chèvre in a little parcel of foil and place in the freezer for up to 2 hours until hard.

Place the black olives, half the garlic, and 1/3 cup olive oil in a blender and blend until coarsely chopped. Set aside.

Cook the fava beans in boiling salted water for 4–5 minutes and then drain. Using thumbs and forefinger push out the inner beans from the tough outer skin.

Heat the remaining oil in a nonstick skillet, add the remaining garlic, the arugula, fava beans, and tarragon, and cook together for 1 minute until the arugula begins to wilt. Add the vinegar, toss together, and season.

Lightly toast the ciabatta slices on both sides under the broiler and then smear one side with black olive oil. Dress each slice with the wilted arugula and bean mix and place on four serving plates. Remove the cheese from the freezer and, using a small grater, finely grate the iced cheese all over the top of each crostini. Serve immediately.

PG TIPS   I often vary this dish using artichokes instead of fava beans. A little trickle of truffle oil makes a wonderful addition.

Salad of hearts of palm, beets, and asparagus
with pomegranate dressing

Pomegranates are, I admit, one of the most challenging of fruits for any cook, but with a little patience in their preparation, they make a wonderful, colorful addition to salads. Hearts of palm can be purchased from good delicatessens and supermarkets.

2 medium-size beets

2 tablespoons olive oil

16 asparagus tips, trimmed

4 hearts of palm (canned), sliced lengthwise

2 red chicory, leaves separated

6 tablespoons watercress, stems removed

10 fresh basil leaves

2 tablespoons pistachio nuts, roughly chopped

for the pomegranate dressing

3/4 cup fresh orange juice

1 tablespoon fresh lemon juice

1 tablespoon white wine vinegar

2 tablespoons mild olive oil

1 tablespoon vegetable oil

1 fresh pomegranate

salt and freshly ground black pepper

Preheat the oven to 350°F. Wash the beets, drizzle with olive oil, and wrap them in foil. Place on a cookie sheet and bake in the oven for 1 hour or until just tender. Remove and cool slightly before peeling and then cut each one into ten wedges. Cook the asparagus in boiling salted water for 1 minute, drain, and then refresh in cold water.

For the dressing, place the orange juice and lemon juice in a small pan and cook over a moderate heat until the liquid has reduced by half and become slightly syrupy. Pour into a bowl and leave to cool. When cool, stir in the vinegar and whisk in both oils. Cut the pomegranate in half horizontally and then squeeze out the fruit in the palm of your hand to release the inner seeds, removing any bitter yellow membrane. Add the seeds and the juice to the dressing and season to taste.

Place all the salad ingredients in a bowl, pour over the dressing, and toss the contents lightly together. Place on four serving plates, drizzle over any excess dressing, and serve.

Roquefort-stuffed fig salad
with port vinaigrette and frozen avocado cream

Blue cheese and figs have a natural affinity—the balance of salty cheese
and sweet fruit works wonderfully together. This salad is one of my
favorite ways to use figs and makes an interesting dish or talking point
when prepared for a dinner party, the combination of hot and cold
particularly successful.

for the avocado cream

3/4 cup sugar
2 avocados (preferably Haas variety)
1 cup dry white wine
juice of 1/2 lemon
4 tablespoons heavy cream

for the salad

8 large figs
1/4 pound roquefort cheese
1 tablespoon honey
1 teaspoon truffle oil (optional)
Olive oil
6 tablespoons young arugula leaves
6 tablespoons watercress, any tough stems removed
1 avocado, peeled, pitted and cut into small dice
1/2 cup spiced pecan nuts (see PG TIPS)

for the port vinaigrette

2 tablespoons olive oil
1 shallot, finely chopped
1/2 cup port
3 tablespoons balsamic vinegar
1 tablespoon honey
juice of 1/2 lemon
salt and freshly ground black pepper

For the avocado cream (best made a day in advance), place the sugar and 1/4 cup water in a pan, bring to a boil, and simmer for 1 minute to make a light syrup. Leave to cool. Peel and remove the stone from the avocados, cut the flesh into pieces. Place them in a food processor with the syrup, white wine, and lemon juice and blend until smooth. Add the cream, then transfer to an ice-cream maker and churn according to the manufacturer's instructions. Freeze overnight until required.

Remove a third off the top of each fig and, using a melon baller or teaspoon, scoop out a little of the flesh from the center of each fig, taking care not to destroy their shape. Mix together the cheese, the scooped out flesh, honey, and truffle oil, then stuff each fig with the mixture and replace the top back on the figs. Set aside.

For the port vinaigrette, heat the olive oil in a pan, add the shallot, and cook for 30 seconds. Add the port, vinegar, honey, and lemon juice and boil for 1 minute. Season to taste, pass through a sieve to remove lumps, and keep warm.

Preheat the oven to 425°F. Place the figs on a baking dish, drizzle over a little olive oil, and place in the oven to bake for 5–6 minutes or until just softened.

Toss the arugula and watercress leaves with the diced avocado, spiced nuts, and warm port dressing. Transfer the salad to serving plates. Place two stuffed figs alongside and a scoop of the avocado cream. Drizzle over a little more warm dressing and serve immediately.

PG TIPS   Spiced pecans are great for salads and easy to prepare. Simply heat some corn syrup or honey in a thick nonstick pan, add the pecan nuts and a pinch of cayenne pepper. Lightly caramelize together until golden and sticky in texture, then remove and cool them. When they are cold they will be hard and crunchy in texture. These nuts can be made in advance and are best kept in an airtight container or a cookie tin which will stop them from going soft.

Mojo criolla vegetable salad

I love the punchy flavors in this Latin American-style salad—the tangy piquant dressing beautifully matched with grilled sweet vegetables and buttery avocado.

for the mojo criolla dressing

2 garlic cloves, crushed

1 hot red chili, deseeded and finely chopped

1 teaspoon cumin seeds, toasted

1/2 cup extra-virgin olive oil

3 tablespoons fresh orange juice

2 teaspoons sherry vinegar

1 teaspoon tomato ketchup

salt and freshly ground black pepper

1/2 cup olive oil

2 large red bell peppers, deseeded and cut into thick strips

2 large yellow bell peppers, deseeded and cut into thick strips

12 baby corn

6 small zucchini, halved lengthwise

12 asparagus tips

9 baby leeks, trimmed

4 palm hearts (canned), cut into long batons

1 tablespoon superfine capers

1 avocado, peeled, pitted, and cut into 1/3 inch dice

For the dressing, place the garlic, chili, cumin seeds, and a little salt in a mortar and crush with a pestle to a smooth paste. Heat the olive oil in a pan and, when hot, add the garlic paste. Remove from the heat and leave to stand for 5 minutes, before adding the orange juice, vinegar, and tomato ketchup. Season to taste, leave to cool, and refrigerate until needed.

Heat a ridged skillet until smoking. Drizzle in the olive oil and fry the peppers and baby corn for 5 minutes on each side or until the skins are blistered and charred. Transfer the peppers to a bowl, lightly cover with plastic wrap and leave to steam for 20 minutes. Peel the peppers and place in a large bowl.

Place the remaining vegetables on the skillet and fry until cooked and lightly charred. Place all the vegetables in a bowl, then add a little dressing to the vegetables and toss gently together. Add the capers and diced avocado and toss again. Place in a huge pile, drizzle over the remaining dressing, and serve at room temperature.

Lasagne salad
with artichokes, avocado, fennel, and mozzarella

The ultimate upscale pasta salad, thin stacked layers of pasta encasing a delicious salad of artichoke, buttery avocado, and fennel. Store-bought pasta sheets could be substituted if necessary.

1 teaspoon coriander seeds

pinch of fresh saffron

1 head of fennel, peeled and cut into 1cm strips

1/2 pound prepared pasta dough (see PG TIPS page 112)

olive oil

1 avocado, peeled, pitted and cut into 1/2 inch dice

3 plum tomatoes, deseeded and cut into small dice

1 red onion, peeled and thinly sliced

1/2 cup marinated baby artichokes in oil, drained and oil reserved

1/4 pound mozzarella, cut into 1/3 inch dice

5 tablespoons watercress, tough stems removed

2 tablespoons shiso cress

3 tablespoons corn salad (mâche or lambs lettuce)

salt, freshly ground black pepper, and nutmeg

for the dressing

1 small free-range egg yolk

1/4 teaspoon Dijon mustard

1 garlic clove, crushed

1 tablespoon balsamic vinegar

5 tablespoons reserved artichoke oil (see above)

lemon juice

salt and freshly ground black pepper

Bring 3/4 cup water to a boil in a small pan with the coriander seeds and saffron. Add the fennel and cook for 2–3 minutes, remove it, and leave to cool. Reduce the cooking liquid by half. Set aside.

For the dressing, whisk the egg yolk, mustard, garlic, and vinegar in a bowl, then slowly add the reserved artichoke oil and lemon juice and season to taste. Finally add the reserved fennel broth.

For the pasta, roll out the dough several times until the machine is at its thinnest setting. Cut into twelve neat rectangles, approximately 5 inches x 4 inches. You may need to pass the dough through again to obtain all you need. Cook the pasta sheets in a large pan of boiling salted water for 1–2 minutes, then remove them carefully with a slotted spoon into a bowl of iced water. Drain well, dry them in a clean towel, and lay them out on a clean work surface. Season them with a little salt, pepper, and nutmeg and brush them with a little olive oil.

Place the avocados, tomatoes, onion, artichokes, cooked fennel, and diced mozzarella in a bowl and pour over a little of the prepared dressing. Toss gently together and season to taste.

To serve, lay one sheet of pasta on each serving place, top with some salad, sprinkle over the watercress, shiso, and corn salad, then more pasta, more of the artichoke salad, and finally a layer of pasta. Drizzle over a little more dressing. Prepare all four salads in this manner. Serve at room temperature.

Summer ruby salad

This stunning ruby-colored salad is one of my favorite summertime preparations—a combination of sweet and peppery flavors. I always prefer to cook my own beet, although it's fine to use the cooked varieties sold packed in stores and supermarkets. However, be sure not to buy the pickled variety.

for the dressing

4 tablespoons raspberry or red wine vinegar

¹/2 teaspoon Dijon mustard

1 teaspoon maple syrup

6 tablespoons mild olive oil

salt and freshly ground black pepper

2 large cooked beets (see page 46), peeled and cut into ¹/3 inch dice

1 red onion, thinly sliced

8 red radishes

2 cups watermelon, cut into ¹/3 inch dice

2 cups red cabbage, very thinly sliced

20 fresh purple basil leaves

3 tablespoons edible purple flowers (borage, lavender, pansies etc.)

salt and freshly ground black pepper

For the dressing, whisk together all the ingredients in a bowl and season to taste.

Place all the salad ingredients in another bowl, pour over the dressing, season to taste, and toss together. Place attractively on four serving plates and serve immediately.

PG TIPS   Diced buffalo mozzarella or chèvre makes a good addition to this salad. I also serve the salad dressed in a horseradish crème fraîche dressing, made by whisking together 1 tablespoon of sherry vinegar with 1 tablespoon of creamed horseradish, ¹/2 cup olive oil, 3 tablespoons of crème fraîche, and seasoning.

Salad of chickpeas, cauliflower, and apricots
with roasted bulgur bhel puri

Bhel puri are a savory snack served as a street food in Mumbai in India and are deliciously tasty. The idea came to me to create a salad of sorts with this in mind. The street vendors there have mastered the art of preparing different bhel (snacks) for generations. This is somewhat of a heretical variation with chickpeas, cauliflower, and apricots, but the results are wonderful—a sweet yogurt dressing completes the dish. Puffed rice, Bombay spice mix, and chat masala are available from Indian stores.

2 tablespoons olive oil

1 small onion, chopped

$1/8$ teaspoon turmeric powder

1 garlic clove, crushed

1 small cauliflower, cut into small florets

$1 1/4$ cups bulgur (cracked wheat)

$1/2$ teaspoon cumin seeds

2 cups cooked chickpeas (canned are fine), drained

$1/3$ cup ready-to-eat dried apricots, chopped

$1/3$ cup roasted cashew nuts

2 tablespoons pumpkin seeds

2 tablespoons puffed rice

1 packet Bombay spice mix

$1/2$ teaspoon chat masala

2 tablespoons fresh cilantro leaves

for the dressing

3 tablespoons tamarind paste

1 tablespoon brown sugar

1 small green chili, finely chopped

$1/2$ teaspoon cumin powder

2 tablespoons chopped fresh mint

$1/2$ cup natural yogurt

juice of $1/2$ lemon

Heat the oil in a large skillet and, when warm, add the onion and cook until lightly softened. Add the turmeric powder, garlic, and cauliflower and mix well. Add a little water, cover with a lid, and cook over a gentle heat for 10–12 minutes, until the cauliflower is just cooked, retaining its shape. Remove to a bowl and leave to cool.

Clean out the skillet and heat it again, until hot this time, then add the bulgur wheat and cumin seeds and toss them constantly until they are golden and toasted. Transfer to a bowl, pour over $2 1/2$ cups water, cover with plastic wrap, and leave to soak for 15–20 minutes, then remove the plastic wrap and leave to cool.

For the dressing, combine the tamarind paste and brown sugar with $2/3$ cup water in a small pan and heat until the sugar has melted. Add the chopped chili and the cumin powder, simmer for 5 minutes, and then remove to a bowl to cool. When cool, add the mint, yogurt, and lemon juice.

Add the soaked bulghur to the cauliflower, then add the chickpeas, chopped apricots, cashew nuts, pumpkin seeds, and finally the puffed rice and Bombay mix. Season with a little chat masala, then pour over the sweet yogurt dressing, and toss together. Place on four serving plates and scatter over the cilantro leaves. Serve immediately.

Egg salad
with peanut curry dressing

During my short time promoting and cooking in the Far East, I must have tasted probably a dozen variations of Gado Gado, a Thai-inspired salad of crispy vegetables in a peanut curry dressing, apparently now popular all over southern Asia. This is a sister version, made with hard-boiled eggs and a spicier accent on the sauce.

for the peanut curry dressing

3/4 cup coconut milk

1/2 garlic clove, crushed

3 tablespoons crunchy peanut butter

1 tablespoon sweet chili sauce

juice of 1/2 lime

good pinch of curry powder

1 teaspoon vegetarian fish sauce (nuoc mam chay) – optional

4 free-range eggs

1/2 pound small new potatoes

1 carrot, peeled and sliced

3 ounces French string beans

2 ounces beansprouts

1/2 cucumber, cut into 1/5 inch matchstick lengths

1 small iceburg lettuce, trimmed and shredded

3 tablespoons watercress, stems trimmed

5 tablespoons fresh cilantro leaves

2 tablespoons crispy fried shallots (see PG TIPS)

For the dressing, bring the coconut milk to a boil in a small pan, stir in the remaining ingredients, and simmer for 5 minutes until the peanut butter has melted and the mixture has thickened. Leave to cool to room temperature.

Cook the eggs in a pan of boiling water for 8–10 minutes until hard-boiled, then refresh them under cold water before shelling. Cut them in half and set aside.

In separate pans, cook the potatoes, carrot, and beans, keeping the carrot and beans quite crunchy in texture. The potatoes should be cooked through, drained, then thickly sliced. Refresh all the vegetables in cold water and dry them.

Toss the vegetables, beansprouts, cucumber, and salad leaves together in a bowl and place on four serving plates. Top with two halves of egg per person, pour over the spiced peanut curry dressing, and serve, sprinkled with crispy fried shallots.

PG TIPS   In Thailand and the Philippines, many dishes are topped with crispy fried shallots, which add not only flavor but texture to the dish. To prepare them, simply heat some vegetable oil to 320°F, thinly slice the shallots, and dip them in the hot oil until golden. Remove with a slotted spoon onto paper towels, leave to drain and crisp up, and use as required.

Smoked paprika feta salad
with peppers, date cigarillos, and sweet lemon dressing

A Middle Eastern-inspired salad with a combination of salty and sweet flavors. The date cigarillos can be prepared in advance and frozen until needed. Some fresh figs are also great added to this salad. Sumac is a tangy seasoning that has been used for thousands of years by Middle Eastern cooks, often as a replacement for lemon or vinegar.

for the cigarillos

2 sheets phyllo pastry

1 cup ready-to-eat dates, chopped finely

vegetable oil for deep-frying

for the salad

2 tablespoons olive oil

4 red bell peppers, halved and deseeded

1/2 pound feta cheese, cut into large dice

1 teaspoon smoked paprika

12 black olives

1 red onion, thinly sliced

2 tablespoons flaked almonds, toasted

for the dressing

2 lemons, halved

3 tablespoons argan oil (or olive oil)

pinch of good cinnamon

1/2 garlic clove, crushed

pinch of sumac (optional)

2 tablespoons chopped fresh mint

1 teaspoon superfine sugar

salt and freshly ground black pepper

For the date cigarillos, lay a sheet of phyllo pastry onto a work surface or board and cut into four equal rectangles, keeping the remainder of the pastry covered with a damp dish towel to prevent it drying out. Lay a good spoonful of the dates at the short end of one of the phyllo rectangles. Tightly roll up the pastry, tucking the sides in as you near the end to securely encase the filling. Seal the last 2 inches of the cigarillo with a little cold water. Repeat until the filling and pastry are used up. Set aside.

Heat a ridged skillet until very hot, brush the skillet with the olive oil. Cut each pepper half into three strips lengthwise. Place on the skillet and cook until tender and slightly charred, turning them regularly. Remove and peel off their skin. Leave to cool, then transfer to a bowl.

For the dressing, place the lemon halves under the broiler and cook for 2–3 minutes until the lemon is slightly cooked and lightly charred. Remove and cool slightly, then squeeze the juice from the lemons into a bowl, and add the remaining ingredients; season to taste.

Dust the feta pieces lightly with smoked paprika. Add the olives, onion, and almonds to the pepper, pour over a little of the lemon dressing, and season to taste. Place the salad on a serving plate, top with the paprika-dusted feta, and drizzle over the remaining dressing.

Heat the vegetable oil to 350°F, drop the date cigarillos into the hot oil and cook for 1 minute until golden and crispy. Remove from the oil and drain on paper towels. Garnish the salad with two cigarillos per person and serve.

Pasta and grains

Simply by taking a trip around any good food

store or shop these days, you will see the vast

range of pasta and grains now available for

vegetarians to expand their menu options.

Whether for a simple midweek meal or an

impressive dinner party course, pasta and grain

dishes are generally simple and quick to make

and look wonderful. Most of these recipes can

be used interchangeably, using the different

combinations of ingredients so you can enjoy

even more recipes than you bargained for!

Three grain risotto
with pan-roasted salsify, shiitake mushrooms, and vanilla-hazelnut foam

The idea of using different grains in the risotto stems from a similar dish served at the superb Union Square Café in New York. The combination of the grains adds a wonderful nutty flavor and, of course, it is very healthy. I sometimes add fontina to the risotto instead of parmesan and mascarpone cheese.

$^1/_3$ cup wild rice, soaked overnight

3 tablespoons spelt

$^1/_2$ stick unsalted butter

1 tablespoon olive oil

$^1/_2$ pound salsify, peeled

$1^1/_4$ cups shiitake mushrooms, thickly sliced

2 shallots, finely chopped

$^1/_4$ cup vialano nano risotto rice (or similar variety)

4 tablespoons dry white wine

$2^1/_4$ cups good vegetable broth, hot

2 tablespoons freshly grated castelli vegetalia
   (parmesan-style cheese)

1 tablespoon mascarpone cheese

2 tablespoons heavy cream

salt and freshly ground black pepper

for the vanilla-hazelnut foam

2 tablespoons whole hazelnuts

$^1/_2$ cup skim milk

$^1/_2$ cup heavy cream

4 tablespoons dry white wine

$^1/_2$ vanilla bean, split and seeds removed (see PG TIPS)

3 tablespoons unsalted butter

salt and freshly ground black pepper

Cook the wild rice in boiling water for 50–60 minutes or until tender. In a separate pan, cook the spelt in boiling water for 30 minutes or until tender. Drain both grains and set aside.

Heat 2 tablespoons butter and the olive oil in a pan, add the salsify, and cook over a moderate heat for 4–5 minutes until golden all over. Add the shiitake mushrooms and $^1/_2$ cup water, cover with a lid, reduce the heat, and cook for a further 10 minutes. Keep warm.

Heat a further 1 tablespoon butter in a heavy-based pan, add the shallots, and cook for 1 minute. Add the risotto rice, the cooked wild rice, and spelt and stir well to coat with the butter. Add the white wine and boil for 1 minute. Over a moderate heat, add the hot vegetable broth a ladleful at a time, only adding more once each quantity has been absorbed. The rice should be just tender, but still retain a little bite when cooked—about 25 minutes in all. Remove from the heat, add the remaining butter, the cheeses, and cream and season to taste. The finished risotto should be fairly loose without being too sloppy.

For the foam, place the hazelnuts and milk in a food processor and blend until smooth. Transfer to a small pan, add the cream, wine, and vanilla seeds and bring to a boil. Reduce the heat and simmer for 2 minutes, then strain through a fine strainer. Add the butter a little at a time and blend with a handheld blender until foaming in texture; season to taste. Place the risotto on four serving plates or bowls, top with the salsify and mushrooms, and spoon over the hazelnut foam. Serve immediately.

PG TIPS To remove the inner seeds from a fresh vanilla bean, cut the bean in half lengthwise, then using the back of a small knife, carefully scrape out the black inner seeds. Use the pods to make vanilla sugar by placing them in a sealed jar with superfine sugar—wonderful in dessert recipes.

Roasted butternut squash and chèvre risotto
with almond crumble

I have more risotto recipes in my repertoire than I can mention, but this one is my favorite. The smoky flavor of the roasted squash is offset beautifully by the creaminess of the goat's cheese.

2^1/2 cups good vegetable broth

1 stick of cinnamon

1 small bay leaf

3 fresh sage leaves

2 tablespoons olive oil

2 shallots, finely chopped

1^1/3 cups vialano nano risotto rice (or similar variety)

1 pound butternut squash, peeled and cut into large dice

^{1}/2 cup dry white wine

3 tablespoons heavy cream

3 ounces mild chèvre, crumbled or grated

1 tablespoon unsalted butter

salt and freshly ground black pepper

for the almond crumble

4 amaretti biscuits

2 teaspoons unsalted butter

^{1}/2 teaspoon ground cinnamon

Place the vegetable broth, cinnamon, bay leaf, and sage in a large pan, simmer gently for 10–15 minutes and then strain.

Heat the olive oil in a heavy-based pan, add the shallots, and cook over a gentle heat to lightly color and caramelize them. Add the rice and the butternut squash and toss together carefully. Pour over the white wine and stir until it has been absorbed. Over a moderate heat, add the fragrant broth a ladleful at a time, only adding more once each quantity has been absorbed. The rice should be just tender, but still retain a little bite when cooked—about 20–25 minutes in all. Add the cream, chèvre, and butter and fold gently into the rice. The finished risotto should be fairly loose without being sloppy. Adjust the seasoning to taste.

For the almond crumble, place the amaretti biscuits, butter, and cinnamon in a food processor and blend for a few seconds to form small pieces.

Transfer the risotto to four deep serving bowls, sprinkle the almond crumble over the top, and serve immediately.

Walnut risotto
with brown butter and taleggio crostini

An unusual way to finish a superb risotto. After preparing the risotto in the normal manner, crisp bread slices draped with fontina cheese are layered on top. A fragrant butter is poured over the cheese, heating it sufficiently to melt it. This dish is typical of the Val d'Aosta region of Italy. Taleggio cheese is one of Italy's most prized and loved cheeses and is available from good delicatessens.

1 stick unsalted butter

2 shallots, finely chopped

1/2 garlic clove, crushed

1 1/3 cups vialano nano risotto rice (or similar variety)

4 tablespoons dry white wine

3 cups good vegetable broth, hot

2/3 cup walnuts, coarsely chopped

3 tablespoons watercress leaves

1/2 small crusty French bread, cut into 2 inch thick slices

1/4 pound taleggio cheese, thinly sliced

3 tablespoons unsalted butter

salt and freshly ground black pepper

Heat the butter in a heavy-based pan over a moderate heat, add the shallots and garlic, and cook for 1 minute until softened but not colored. Add the rice and stir until well coated with the butter. Pour over the white wine and stir until it has been absorbed. Over a moderate heat, add the hot vegetable broth a ladleful at a time, only adding more once each quantity has been absorbed. The rice should be just tender, but still retain a little bite when cooked—about 20–25 minutes in all. Add the walnuts and watercress and season to taste.

Toast the bread until golden on both sides. Transfer the rice to four deep serving bowls. Top each risotto with bread slices then drape the taleggio over the bread.

In a small skillet, heat the butter until it foams, becomes nutty in fragrance and turns hazelnut in color. Quickly spoon over the cheese and leave for 30 seconds to allow the cheese to soften before serving.

Wild rice and parsnip suppli
with crushed cauliflower and cherry jus

"Suppli" is the Italian word for rice fritters. I also recommend serving this
dish with some roasted wild or portobello mushrooms. The fresh sage
can be replaced with rosemary or chopped flat-leaf parsley.

1/3 cup wild rice, soaked overnight and drained

2 tablespoons unsalted butter

1 onion, finely chopped

6 sage leaves, roughly chopped

2 parsnips, peeled and grated

2/3 cup vialano nano risotto rice (or similar variety)

3 3/4 cups good vegetable broth, hot

2 tablespoons freshly grated castelli vegetalia
  (parmesan-style cheese)

1 cup fresh white breadcrumbs

4 tablespoons all-purpose flour

2 free-range eggs, lightly beaten

1 cauliflower, cut into small florets

5 tablespoons olive oil

salt and freshly ground black pepper

for the cherry jus

2 tablespoons demerara sugar

4 tablespoons sherry vinegar (or red wine vinegar)

1/2 cup port wine

3/4 cup vegetarian jus (see page 189)

1/3 cup dried cherries

1 tablespoon unsalted butter, chilled and cut into
  small pieces

Cook the wild rice in plenty of boiling salted water for 40–45 minutes or until tender.
Drain well and dry.

Melt the butter in a heavy-based pan, add the onion and half the sage, and cook
over a low heat for about 3–4 minutes until soft. Add the parsnips and risotto rice
and cook together for 1–2 minutes. Over a moderate heat, add the hot vegetable
broth a ladleful at a time, only adding more once each quantity has been absorbed.
The rice should be just tender, but still retain a little bite when cooked—about 20–25
minutes in all. Remove from the heat, add the cheese, cooked rice, breadcrumbs,
and remaining sage, and mix well before turning out onto a cookie sheet. Leave
to cool.

Divide the mixture into eight and shape into cakes. Dip them in flour, then into
the beaten egg, and refrigerate until required. (The cakes can be made to this stage a
day in advance.)

For the cherry jus, place the sugar and vinegar in a pan and lightly caramelize
together until golden. Add the port wine, vegetarian jus, and dried cherries and simmer
for 10 minutes over a low heat. Add the chilled butter and swirl it into the sauce.
Keep hot.

Cook the cauliflower florets in boiling water until tender, drain them well, add
2 tablespoons of the olive oil and a little seasoning, and crush them lightly with a fork.
Keep hot.

Cook the cakes in a large skillet in the remaining olive oil for 2–3 minutes on each
side until golden. Drain on kitchen paper. Place two cooked cakes on each serving
plate on a bed of crushed cauliflower and pour around some of the cherry jus.
Serve immediately.

Goan chickpea risotto
with cashew nuts and coconut yogurt

Here is a tongue-in-cheek look at an Asian-style risotto that materialized one night at home, during a hunger spell. It was rather good and so I decided to share it with you.

for the mild curry paste

4 teaspoons garam masala

2 tablespoons mild curry powder

$^1/2$ cup ghee or clarified butter (see PG TIPS page 171)

2 shallots, finely chopped

2 garlic cloves, crushed

$^1/4$ pound baby spinach leaves

1$^1/4$ cups vialano nano risotto rice (or similar variety)

2$^1/2$ cups good vegetable broth, hot

2 cups cooked chickpeas (canned are fine), drained

3 tablespoons cashew nuts, toasted and roughly chopped

$^1/4$ cup raisins, soaked in water for 30 minutes and drained

1 tablespoon fresh cilantro leaves

$^1/2$ cup coconut yogurt to serve (see page 135)

For the curry paste, place the garam masala and curry powder in a bowl and stir in 2 tablespoons of water. Set aside.

Melt the ghee or butter in a heavy-based pan, add the shallots and garlic and cook for 2–3 minutes until softened. Add the spinach and cook for 1 minute. Add the rice, then stir well to coat with the vegetables and butter. Stir in the curry paste and mix well. Over a moderate heat, add the hot vegetable broth a ladleful at a time, only adding more once each quantity has been absorbed. The rice should be just tender, but still retain a little bite when cooked—about 20–25 minutes. Add the chickpeas, cashews, raisins, and half the cilantro and cook for a further 1 minute. Divide the rice among four serving plates, drizzle over a little of the coconut yogurt, and scatter over the remaining cilantro. Serve immediately.

Pumpkin and aduki bean biryani

There are many types of biryani, flavored with spices and cooked with meat or vegetables. It is one of the great classics of the Indian kitchen. This recipe is a variation from my friend Janmejoy Sen, restaurant chef of the Imperial New Delhi. He says the secret of a good biryani is not only in the spices, but cooking the rice in two stages to keep it light and fluffy. A mint chutney completes a great dish and can be made in advance and kept in the fridge.

1 cup aduki (or adzuki) beans

vegetable oil for shallow frying

2 onions, very thinly sliced

4 garlic cloves, crushed

2 inch piece of fresh ginger, peeled and chopped

1³/4 cups basmati rice, rinsed and drained

1³/4 pounds ghee or clarified butter (see PG TIPS page 171)

2 tablespoons biryani curry paste

2 teaspoons ground cardamom

¹/2 teaspoon chili powder

¹/2 teaspoon ground turmeric

3 cups pumpkin, peeled and cut into large pieces

1 teaspoon garam masala

juice of 1 lemon

¹/2 cup flaked almonds, toasted

mint chutney (see PG TIPS)—optional

Rinse the aduki beans under cold water, place in a pan, cover with water, and cook over a moderate heat for 40–45 minutes or until tender. Drain and set aside.

Heat the vegetable oil in a large pan or skillet and, when it reaches 325°F, add the thinly sliced onions and fry until golden and slightly crisp. Remove with a slotted spoon and drain on paper towels.

Blend the garlic and ginger to a paste in a blender. Place the rice into a pan of 2¹/2 cups boiling water, cook for 10–12 minutes, and then drain.

Melt the ghee or clarified butter in a large heavy-based pan, add half the fried onion, the garlic, and ginger paste and cook over a moderate heat for 2 minutes. Add the biryani paste, cardamom, chili powder, and turmeric and cook for a further 2 minutes. Add the pumpkin and aduki beans, along with 1¹/4 cups water, cover, and cook for about 10 minutes until the pumpkin is just tender. Add the half-cooked rice, cover with a lid, and reduce the heat to its lowest setting. Allow the steam to cook the rice for a further 8–10 minutes until tender and fluffy. Remove the lid, add the garam masala and lemon juice, and toss well together. Transfer to a serving dish, top with the remaining crispy fried onions and the toasted flaked almonds, and serve with the mint chutney, if desired.

PG TIPS   For a simple Indian-style mint chutney, blend together until smooth a handful of mint leaves, 1 teaspoon of sugar, ¹/2 cup natural yogurt, 1 teaspoon of tamarind paste and 1 deseeded green chili. Season with a little cumin and refrigerate until needed. This chutney will keep for 2 days in the fridge, when it will begin to lose its color. This chutney is good served with all kinds of Indian-style dishes.

Honey-roasted vegetables
with cumin and fig couscous, and olive sauce

Every honey is different, the flavor and strength determined by the flowers that the bees visit. Cheap brands all tend to taste the same, so it is worth paying that little bit extra for a good one.

for the olive sauce
1/2 cup milk

1 garlic clove, crushed

3 tablespoons ground almonds

1 cup fresh white breadcrumbs

1/3 cup pitted black olives, chopped

6 tablespoons olive oil

4 tablespoons yogurt

salt and freshly ground black pepper

for the honey-roasted vegetables
4 tablespoons good quality honey

juice and zest of 1 lemon

1 eggplant, cut into 1/2 inch dice

1 red onion, cut into wedges

2 zucchini, cut into 1/2 inch dice

2 red bell peppers, cut into 1/2 inch dice

1 yellow bell pepper, cut into 1/2 inch dice

olive oil

2 1/2 cups good vegetable broth, hot

salt and freshly ground pepper

for the cumin and fig couscous
1 3/4 cups couscous

1 teaspoon ground cumin

2 cups good vegetable broth, hot

4 ripe but firm figs, cut into wedges

2 tablespoons chopped fresh mint

2 tablespoons chopped fresh flat-leaf parsley

Preheat the oven to 450°F. For the olive sauce, place the milk, garlic, almonds, and breadcrumbs in a food processor and blend to a smooth purée. Add the olives and blend for a further 20–30 seconds. With the motor running, gently pour in the the olive oil through the funnel at the top and continue blending until smooth. Remove to a bowl, season to taste (taking care not to add too much salt as the olives are already salty in flavor), and stir in the yogurt. Refrigerate until needed.

For the vegetables, place the honey, lemon juice, and zest in a roasting pan and add the vegetables. Drizzle over some olive oil, toss well together, and season lightly. Put in the oven and roast for 15 minutes until lightly caramelized, tossing them from time to time to ensure even cooking. Pour over the vegetable broth and cook for a further 20–25 minutes until the vegetables are cooked and the liquid in the tray is thick and caramelized.

Meanwhile, place the couscous in a shallow dish. Add the cumin, pour over the hot vegetable broth to cover, and stir well. Cover and leave to stand for 5–6 minutes before separating the grains with a fork. Add the fig wedges and chopped herbs. Serve with the roasted vegetables on top, drizzle over the pan juices and olive sauce. Serve immediately.

Buckwheat spaetzle
with cavalo nero, roasted chanterelles, and chestnuts

Spaetzle—tender little morsels that are like a cross between a noodle and a dumpling—are common to Austrian, German, and Swiss cuisine. They are excellent for absorbing creamy sauces as in this recipe. Cavolo nero (black cabbage) is a wonderful Italian cabbage—replace with Savoy cabbage if unavailable.

for the spaetzle

2 cups all-purpose flour

3/4 cup buckwheat flour

6 free-range eggs, beaten

iced water

salt and freshly ground black pepper

2 tablespoons unsalted butter

1 tablespoon mild olive oil

1 shallot, finely chopped

1 garlic clove, crushed

1/2 pound chanterelle mushrooms, cleaned

1 tablespoon chopped fresh flat-leaf parsley

3 ounces vacuum-packed chestnuts

1 1/2 cups cavalo nero, finely shredded

1/2 cup heavy cream

1 tablespoon grated vegetarian Swiss cheese

1 tablespoon truffle oil

For the spaetzle, sift the flour and a little salt into a large bowl and add the buckwheat flour. Make a well in the center, tip in the beaten eggs, and, using your hands or a wooden spoon, mix them into the flour with enough water to form a thick but runny batter.

Bring a large pan of salted water to a boil and top the pan with a large-holed colander (ensuring the colander does not touch the water). Pour in a little of the batter and, using a scraper or flat spatula, push the batter through the colander into the water. When the noodles rise to the surface—after about 1 minute—remove them with a slotted spoon into iced water. Prepare all the spaetzle in the same way. Drain well in a colander and dry in a cloth.

For the vegetables, heat the butter and oil in a large skillet over a gentle heat, add the shallot and garlic, and cook until tender. Raise the heat, add the chanterelles, parsley, and chestnuts, and fry until golden. Add the cavalo nero, toss together, add 1/2 cup water, and cook for 3–4 minutes.

Throw in the spaetzle, toss with the vegetables, and heat through. Add the cream and cheese and season to taste. Place in a serving dish, drizzle over the truffle oil and serve.

Mee krob

One of my favorite memories during my short time working in Singapore is eating this simple Asian vegetable dish of crunchy cooked vegetables, on top of a bed of crispy rice noodles.

groundnut or vegetable oil for deep-frying

4 ounces rice vermicelli noodles

2 tablespoons vegetable oil

6 shallots, finely sliced

3 garlic cloves, crushed

1 red chili, very thinly sliced

4 ounces firm tofu, cut into $^1/3$ inch dice (optional)

$^1/2$ cup peanuts, chopped

1 small butternut squash, peeled and thinly sliced

1 cup oyster mushrooms, cut into strips

4 large green onions, sliced thinly

1 cup baby corn

$^3/4$ cup French string beans, topped, tailed, and blanched

$^3/4$ cup beansprouts

2 tablespoons palm sugar (or brown sugar)

2 tablespoons rice wine vinegar (or white wine vinegar)

1 teaspoon vegetarian fish sauce (nuoc mam chay)—optional

juice of 1 lime

3 tablespoons fresh cilantro leaves

Heat the oil in a skillet or large pan. When the oil is hot, add the noodles, a few at a time, until puffed up and cooked—only a matter of seconds. Remove with a slotted spoon onto paper towels and drain thoroughly.

Heat a wok or large skillet with 2 tablespoons of vegetable oil, add the shallots and garlic and cook until they turn golden. Add the chili, tofu (if using), peanuts, and vegetables and stir-fry for 2–3 minutes. Add the palm sugar, vinegar, fish sauce, and lime juice and cook for a further 30 seconds. Divide the fried noodles among four serving plates, top with the vegetables, garnish with the cilantro leaves and serve.

Black mushroom fideau

A fideau is a Spanish noodle dish, made using fideos noodles. In this recipe, a collection of assorted wild and cultivated mushrooms cooked in an enriched mushroom broth form the base of the dish.

for the broth

1 pound flat mushrooms

2 teaspoons tomato paste

2 tablespoons mild olive oil

1 onion, chopped

1 garlic clove, crushed

few cilantro stalks

6 cups vegetable broth

2 tablespoons olive oil

1 onion, finely chopped

1 garlic clove, crushed

1 1/2 pounds wild and cultivated mushrooms (i.e. chestnut, trompettes, girolles, shiitake), cleaned and cut into pieces

1/2 teaspoon smoked paprika

6 ounces fideos noodles (or spaghetti)

4 ounces orzo pasta

4 tomatoes, blanched, skinned, and chopped

5 ounces aïoli (garlic mayonnaise)—see PG TIPS

For the base broth, place the flat mushrooms and tomato paste in a food processor and blend to a coarse mush. Heat the olive oil in a pan, add the onion and garlic, and cook for 2–3 minutes. Add the mushroom mixture and cilantro stalks and cook over a high heat for 5 minutes, stirring regularly. Add the vegetable broth and simmer for a further 15 minutes. Strain the broth through a fine strainer and keep hot.

Preheat the oven to 350°F. Heat the olive oil in a casserole dish, add the onions and garlic, and cook for 1 minute. Throw in the mushrooms and smoked paprika and cook over a high heat for 2 minutes. Pour over the hot mushroom broth and bring to a boil. Stir in both pastas and the tomatoes, reduce the heat to a simmer, and cook for 6 minutes. Place in the oven for 5–6 minutes to finish cooking and lightly crisp the surface. Leave to cool slightly. Serve with the aïoli.

PG TIPS   For the aïoli, crush 2 garlic cloves in a mortar. Add 1 egg yolk and mix. Trickle in 3/4 cup olive oil, stirring constantly in the same direction to mix thoroughly. Add a little salt and a dash of lemon juice. The sauce should be thick and glossy.

My fusion noodles

A simple and quick dish to prepare when you are hungry and short of time. The flavors from the Far East and Italy blend well together; remember, it was Marco Polo who allegedly introduced pasta to the Western world, bringing it back from China.

8 ounces Chinese egg noodles

2 tablespoons olive oil

$^1/_2$ garlic clove, crushed

1 red chili, deseeded and finely chopped

1 inch piece of fresh ginger, peeled and chopped

2 cups shiitake mushrooms, thinly sliced

3 tablespoons pesto sauce (see PG TIPS)

serves 6–8

Bring a large pan of water to a boil, add the noodles and cook according to the packet instructions. Drain in a colander and set aside.

Heat the oil in a large frying pan, add the garlic, chili, and ginger and cook for 1 minute. Throw in the shiitake mushrooms and cook for a further 2–3 minutes. Add the cooked noodles and toss with the mushrooms, using a pair of kitchen tongs. Finally, add the pesto sauce and toss again. Place in four serving bowls and serve immediately.

PG TIPS   For homemade pesto, place 5 tablespoons of fresh basil leaves, 2 peeled garlic cloves, 1 tablespoon of pine kernels, 2 tablespoons of finely grated castelli vegetalia (parmesan-style cheese), and a pinch of sugar in a blender. Blend until finely chopped, then drizzle in $^1/_2$ cup good quality olive oil through the funnel and blend until almost smooth. Season to taste.

Sardinian carrot gnocchi
with minted caramelized cipollini onions and leeks

The grain fregola is Sardinia's version of couscous, and is sometimes flavored with saffron. Commercial fregola is getting easier to find at Italian grocers and speciality food stores; it also comes in different sizes, but use the smaller variety for this dish.

1 pound carrots, peeled and left whole

2 cups milk

ground nutmeg

1 1/4 cups fregola (Sardinian semolina or semolina flour)

3 tablespoons freshly grated castelli vegetalia (parmesan-style cheese)—plus more for garnishing

3 free-range egg yolks

2 tablespoons unsalted butter, melted

salt and freshly ground black pepper

for the caramelized onions and leeks

1/2 stick unsalted butter

1 tablespoon superfine sugar

1 pound cipollini onions, peeled

12 baby leeks, cut into 3 inch lengths

1 tablespoon chopped fresh mint

Place the carrots in a pan, cover with water, bring to a boil and simmer for about 25 minutes until just tender. Drain and slice them into 1 inch thick slices. Transfer to a food processor and blend until smooth. Set aside.

Heat the milk together with salt and a little nutmeg. When it boils, stir in the fregola, little by little, stirring constantly with a whisk so that lumps do not form. Once it is all incorporated, add the carrot purée and mix well. Cook on the lowest heat for 15 minutes, stirring from time to time. Remove from the heat, leave to cool for 15 minutes, then vigorously stir in 2 tablespoons cheese and the egg yolks. Spread out the mixture, about 1/2 inch thick, into a well buttered baking dish or tray and leave to cool. Preheat the oven to 425°F.

Using a cookie cutter 2 inches in diameter, cut out disks from the mixture, and place in another well buttered baking dish. Brush them liberally with melted butter, sprinkle over the remaining tablespoon of cheese, and place in the oven for about 15 minutes until the gnocchi begin to brown.

Meanwhile, for the caramelized onions, place the butter and sugar in a pan along with 1 cup water and bring to a boil. Add the cipollini onions, leeks, and mint and cook over a gentle heat until they are cooked and the vegetables lightly caramelized in the mint butter. Place the gnocchi on four serving plates, top with the caramelized vegetables, and drizzle over the remaining cooking juices. Scatter over some cheese and serve immediately.

Purple potato gnocchi
with basil-scented spring vegetables

Gnocchi made with purple potatoes (also known as truffle potatoes) make a strikingly colorful dish. The Provençal-style vegetables make this dish a taste sensation.

for the gnocchi
2 pounds purple potatoes, peeled

2 cups all-purpose flour

1 free-range egg

salt, freshly cracked black pepper, and ground nutmeg

for the vegetables
6 tablespoons extra-virgin olive oil

1 head of fennel, cut into $^1/_3$ inch strips

3$^1/_2$ ounces carrots, cut into $^1/_3$ inch lozenges

3 baby courgettes, cut into $^1/_3$ inch lozenges

$^1/_2$ cup shelled peas (or frozen)

$^1/_4$ cup shelled fava beans

1 garlic clove, crushed

2 firm but ripe tomatoes, blanched, seeded, and chopped

10 fresh basil leaves

salt and freshly ground black pepper

Place the potatoes in a pan, cover with water, bring to a boil and simmer for about 25–30 minutes or until tender. Drain well and dry in a dish towel. Rub the potatoes through a fine strainer into a large bowl. Add the flour and egg and season with salt, pepper, and nutmeg. Mix well together and knead to form a smooth dough. With floured hands, roll the dough into long 1 inch diameter cylinders, then cut into 1 inch pieces. Using a fork, make an indentation on each piece. Place the rolled gnocchi on a floured tray until ready to cook.

For the vegetables, heat half the olive oil in a large pan, add the fennel and cook over a low heat, covered, for 5–6 minutes. Then add the carrots, zucchini, and 2 tablespoons of water and cook for a further 10 minutes or until the vegetables are just tender. Add the peas and fava beans and cook for a further 5 minutes. After cooking there should be about 4 tablespoons of liquid left. Pour in the remaining oil, garlic, and tomatoes and season to taste, then cook for a final 2 minutes. Stir in the basil and keep warm.

Bring a large saucepan of salted water to a boil, reduce the heat, add the gnocchi, and poach for 3–4 minutes or until they rise to the surface of the water. Drain them well. Place the gnocchi in four serving bowls, pour over the vegetables, and season with a little cracked black pepper and serve.

Sweet potato and coconut polenta
with Asian vegetable fricassé

An Asian-Italian twist on polenta, flavored with coconut milk, which
provides the perfect base for the quickly cooked Asian vegetable medley.

1³/4 cups good vegetable broth

1 large sweet potato, peeled and cut into small dice

2¹/2 cups coconut milk

¹/2 stick unsalted butter

1 cup quick-cook polenta

salt and freshly ground black pepper

for the vegetables

2 tablespoons vegetable oil

1 tablespoon unsalted butter

1 garlic clove, crushed

¹/3 inch piece of fresh ginger, peeled and finely chopped

1 cup shiitake mushrooms, sliced

2 zucchini, sliced diagonally

1 small head of broccoli, cut into small florets

¹/4 pound sugar snap peas, sliced diagonally

¹/2 cup good vegetable broth

4 tablespoons sweet chili sauce

serves 6–8

Place the vegetable broth and diced sweet potato in a pan, bring to a boil and simmer for 12–15 minutes until the potato is tender. Transfer to a food processor and blend until smooth. Return to the pan, add the coconut milk and half the butter, and bring to a rolling boil. Pour in the polenta, stirring constantly, lower the heat, and simmer for 5–8 minutes until the polenta comes away from the sides of the pan, with the consistency of wet mashed potato. Stir in the remaining butter, season to taste, and keep warm.

For the vegetables, heat the oil and butter in a wok or skillet over a moderate heat, add the garlic and ginger and cook for 30 seconds. Add the vegetables, toss together for 2 minutes, then add the vegetable broth and sweet chili sauce. Pour the wet polenta onto four serving plates or bowls and top with the vegetables. Serve immediately.

Tomato, spinach, and basil sformatino

An impressive Mediterranean polenta cake, which is light and delicious and full of gutsy flavors. Any leftovers make a great base, pan-fried and then topped with chèvre or mozzarella.

1 litre milk

4 garlic cloves, crushed

1 1/4 cups quick-cook polenta

1 1/2 sticks butter

2 red chilies, deseeded and finely chopped

1 onion, finely chopped

3 ounces fresh spinach leaves

5 tablespoons fresh basil leaves (plus more for garnishing)

2 tablespoons pine nuts, toasted

2/3 cup semidry tomatoes in oil, drained and chopped

2 free-range eggs, separated

salt, freshly ground black pepper, and ground nutmeg

2 pound loaf pan

serves 6–8

Preheat the oven to 350°F. Place the milk and half the garlic in a pan and bring to a boil. Stir in the polenta and cook over a low heat for 2–3 minutes, stirring constantly. Divide the polenta into two equal amounts.

Melt 3/4 stick butter in a skillet, add the remaining garlic, the chilies, onion, and spinach leaves and cook over a high heat for 2–3 minutes until tender and all the liquid from the spinach has evaporated. Add the basil, mix well, then place in a food processor and blend to a coarse purée or chop finely with a knife. Add the mixture to one half of the polenta. Add the pine nuts and chopped semidry tomatoes to the other half of the polenta. Season both polentas to taste with salt, pepper, and a little nutmeg. Mix the egg yolks and whip the whites separately, and add equal amounts of yolk and whites to each polenta.

Heavily grease a loaf pan and then put in alternating layers of both polentas until you reach the top. Tap down to exclude any air. Place in the oven to bake for 12–15 minutes until well risen and golden. Leave to cool slightly before unmolding to allow it to set. Slice into equal portions and place on serving plates.

Melt the remaining butter in a skillet, add some basil and 2 tablespoons of water and cook for 1 minute until emulsified. Pour a little around each slice and serve.

Orecchiette

with chickpeas, broccoli raab, garlic, basil, and olive oil

Orrechiette (or ear-shaped pasta) is made from flavored durum wheat semolina and can be difficult to perfect, especially the shaping technique. Delicatessens seem to sell good quality ones, so it is sometimes not worth making them yourself. For all you enthusiasts and foodies, I include a recipe for fresh orecchiette anyway. If using bought orrechiette you will need 14 ounces for this recipe. If you can't find broccoli raab, then use any kind of greens.

for the orecchiette

$1^1/2$ cups "00" pasta flour

$^1/2$ cup durum wheat semolina

2 tablespoons olive oil

$^3/4$ cup warm water

salt

for the sauce

$^3/4$ pound broccoli raab

7 ounces orrechiette pasta (homemade or bought)

4 tablespoons extra-virgin olive oil

2 garlic cloves, crushed

1 red onion, halved and thinly sliced

pinch of red chili flakes

$1^1/3$ cups cooked chickpeas (canned are fine), drained

10 fresh basil leaves, torn in pieces

6 fresh mint leaves, torn in pieces

freshly grated castelli vegetalia (parmesan-style cheese)—optional

salt and freshly ground black pepper

For the freshly made orrechiette, mix together the flour and semolina and make a well in the center. Add a pinch of salt, the olive oil, and water. Work in the flour from the edges and knead the dough for at least 10 minutes, then place in a lightly floured bowl, cover with a dish towel and leave to stand for 30 minutes. Divide the dough into four and roll into long strips $^1/2$ inch in diameter, then cut each roll into $^1/2$ inch pieces and roll these into balls. Flatten each ball with the thumb so that the dough resembles an earlobe. Place on a floured dish towel, cover and leave to dry for a few hours.

For the sauce, cut the broccoli raab into small florets and the stalk into large pieces. Cook it in plenty of boiling salted water for 4–5 minutes—it should be fairly well cooked. Remove and drain in a colander.

Cook the orrechiette in a large pan of boiling salted water for about 4–5 minutes, remove and drain.

Heat the olive oil in a large skillet, add the garlic, onion, and chili flakes and cook over a low heat for 4–5 minutes or until the onion is tender. Add the orrechiette, cooked broccoli, and chickpeas and gently toss together. Scatter over the herbs, season to taste, and serve. Serve the grated cheese separately if preferred.

Olive polenta

with vegetable gratin and salsa verde

Polenta is a staple of north Italian cookery and, whether served creamy soft or simply grilled, it makes a great base for many wonderful dishes. A good tip for dicing the dolcelatte is to freeze it for 1 hour before cutting.

4 cups good vegetable broth

1³/4 cups quick-cook polenta

2 ounces pitted black olives, finely chopped

2 tablespoons extra-virgin olive oil

1 head of fennel, peeled and cut into wedges

1 small butternut squash, peeled and cut into wedges

1/4 pound dolcelatte cheese, cut into small dice

1 tablespoon pine nuts, toasted

salt and freshly ground black pepper

for the salsa verde

3 tablespoons mixed fresh herbs (basil, mint, flat-leaf parsley), chopped

1 tablespoon capers, rinsed and drained

1 teaspoon Dijon mustard

2 garlic cloves, crushed

1 tablespoon white wine vinegar

1/2 cup extra-virgin olive oil

Preheat the oven to 350°F. Bring the vegetable broth to a boil, pour in the polenta, and keep stirring constantly. Reduce the heat and cook for 5–6 minutes until the mixture thickens and begins to leave the sides of the pan. Stir in the olives.

Grease a cookie sheet with a little olive oil, spread the polenta into a 10 inch square then flatten and level off with a palette knife. Place in the fridge to set.

Blanch the fennel wedges in boiling water for 3–4 minutes, then remove and drain well. Place in a baking dish along with the butternut squash. Drizzle over a little olive oil and season well. Roast in the oven for 15–20 minutes until golden and tender.

For the salsa verde, place all the ingredients except the oil in a blender and blend until combined. Add the oil and blend quickly until blended, keeping it fairly coarse. Preheat a broiler to its highest setting.

Cut the polenta into four large triangles. Brush the triangles with a little olive oil and place under the hot broiler until golden and crusty. Remove the vegetables from the oven and arrange them on the polenta triangles. Top each triangle with some diced dolcelatte and return to the broiler for 2 minutes or until softened.

Serve the vegetable polenta wedges on four serving plates, top with a good spoonful of salsa verde, and garnish with toasted pine nuts.

Rolled wild garlic and pumpkin lasagne
with pesto cream

Wild garlic has a short growing season during the spring months. If
unavailable, chives mixed with a little garlic could be used instead. You
are probably confused by a rolled lasagne, but why not? All the flavors of
a classic lasagne are rolled tightly in this pasta dish to great effect.

1 pound pumpkin (or butternut squash), peeled,
  deseeded, and cut into large pieces
6 tablespoons olive oil
3 tablespoons chopped fresh wild garlic
3/4 cup ricotta cheese, well drained
1 tablespoon heavy cream
4 tablespoons fresh white breadcrumbs
1 quantity of pasta dough made into 12 fresh lasagne
  sheets (see PG TIPS)
2 tablespoons freshly grated castelli vegetalia (parmesan-
  style cheese)
salt and freshly ground black pepper

For the pesto cream
3 tablespoons fresh flat-leaf parsley
2 tablespoons chopped fresh rosemary leaves
2 garlic cloves
1/3 cup blanched almonds
2 tablespoons olive oil
2 tablespoons freshly grated castelli vegetalia
2 tablespoons unsalted butter
2 tablespoons all-purpose flour
1 cup whole or soy milk
4 tablespoons heavy cream
salt and freshly ground black pepper

Preheat the oven to 375°F. Place the pumpkin in a roasting pan, drizzle over the olive oil, and cook in the oven for 25 minutes until the flesh is tender. Remove and leave to cool. Reduce the oven to 300°F.

For the pesto cream, place the herbs, garlic, almonds, and olive oil in a blender and blend to a coarse paste. Stir in the parmesan. Melt the butter in a pan, stir in the flour, cook for 1–2 minutes, then add the milk and bring to a boil. Stir constantly with a whisk, reduce the heat, and simmer for 2–3 minutes until thickened, smooth and glossy. Add the cream and the pesto and stir well; season to taste.

In a bowl, mix the wild garlic, ricotta, cream, pumpkin, and breadcrumbs and season to taste.

Cook the lasagne sheets in boiling water until al dente, then transfer to cold water. Drain and pat the pasta sheets dry with a cloth. Divide the pumpkin mixture equally between the lasagne sheets, making sure it covers them completely. Roll up like a jelly roll, starting from one short end. Lightly grease a suitable ovenproof dish, then arrange the filled lasagne rolls in it. Pour the pesto sauce over the rolls, making sure they are completely covered. Scatter over the parmesan, then place in the oven to bake for 15–20 minutes until the top is golden and slightly crusty on top. Leave to cool a little before serving.

PG TIPS   For the basic pasta recipe, place $2^{1}/_{2}$ cups "00" flour, salt, 2 large beaten eggs, 1 large beaten egg yolk, 1 tablespoon of olive oil, and 1 tablespoon of water in a food processor and blend to mix for a few seconds—it is important not to overwork the dough. Remove from the processor. Knead the dough until soft and pliable, then wrap in plastic wrap and put in the fridge for 1 hour to rest. Roll out the dough and then make it into whatever shape is desired.

For lasagne sheets, use the basic pasta recipe and roll out the dough. Using a sharp knife or plain pasta wheel, cut the dough into 5 inch x 3 inch rectangles.

Crushed potato and bitter greens cannelloni
with white bean and rosemary ragout

In Italy salad greens are often used in pasta dishes to great effect.

for the ragout

1 pound navy beans, soaked overnight and drained

4 tablespoons olive oil

1 small onion, finely chopped

1 carrot, cut into small dice

2 garlic cloves, crushed

pinch of red chili flakes

1 tablespoon chopped fresh rosemary

1/2 cup dry white wine

1 cup semidry tomatoes, chopped

1 1/2 pounds new potatoes, scrubbed

2 tablespoons mild olive oil

2 garlic cloves, crushed

3 tablespoons arugula leaves, stems trimmed

3 tablespoons watercress leaves

6 ounces dolcelatte cheese

12 fresh lasagne sheets (see PG TIPS page 112)

*1/2 cup pesto sauce (bought or homemade—see
   PG TIPS page 103)*

salt, freshly ground black pepper, and ground nutmeg

serves 6–8

For the ragout, place the soaked beans in a large pan, cover with cold water, bring to a boil, reduce the heat, and simmer for 1–1 1/2 hours or until the beans are tender, adding more water if necessary. Drain the beans, reserving their cooking liquid.

Heat half the olive oil in a pan, add the onion, carrot, garlic, chili flakes, and rosemary and cook for 3–4 minutes or until the carrots have softened. Add the white wine and bring to a boil, boil for 2 minutes, before returning the beans and 2/3 cup of the bean cooking liquid to the pan along with the tomatoes. Cook for a further 5 minutes, then stir in the remaining olive oil and season to taste. (This ragout can be made in advance and reheated when needed.)

Cook the new potatoes in boiling salted water for about 20 minutes until tender and then drain. Heat the olive oil in a pan, add the garlic, arugula, and watercress and cook for 1 minute until wilted. Add the potatoes and lightly crush them together. Transfer to a bowl and leave to cool. Once cool, mix with the dolcelatte and season to taste with salt, pepper, and nutmeg.

Cook the lasagne sheets in boiling water until al dente, then transfer to cold water. Drain and pat the pasta sheets dry with a cloth. Season the pasta sheets. Fill them with the potato mixture, roll them up, and brush with a little olive oil. Reheat the cannelloni in a hot oven (or 30 seconds in the microwave on a plate covered with plastic wrap). Reheat the bean ragout and divide among four serving bowls, top each with three cannelloni, drizzle over a little pesto sauce, and serve immediately.

Pumpkin cappelletti
with pumpkin chips and curried carrot cream

These little hats are surprisingly easy to make, but do take a while to prepare. For this recipe I use Asian wonton wrappers, which work extremely well.

for the cappelletti

1 pound piece of pumpkin (or butternut squash), peeled, deseeded and cut into large chunks

1 tablespoon mild olive oil

$1/2$ teaspoon fennel seeds, lightly crushed

1 free-range egg yolk

2 amaretti biscuits, crushed

$1/2$ cup fresh white breadcrumbs

$1/2$ teaspoon Thai red curry paste

2 tablespoons mango chutney, finely chopped

24 wonton wrappers

salt, freshly ground black pepper, and ground nutmeg

for the pumpkin chips

5 ounce wedge of pumpkin, peeled

vegetable oil for deep-frying

for the curried carrot cream

2 carrots, cut into small dice

$3/4$ cup good vegetable broth

1 teaspoon Thai red curry paste

6 tablespoons heavy cream

1 tablespoon unsalted butter

few fresh cilantro leaves, chopped

serves 6–8

Preheat the oven to 400°F. Place the pumpkin in a roasting pan and sprinkle over the oil, fennel seeds, and a little seasoning. Roast for 25 minutes, turning them over once or twice. Remove and leave to cool. Place the pumpkin in a bowl and crush with a fork. Stir in the egg yolk, biscuits, breadcrumbs, curry paste, and mango chutney and mix well; season to taste with salt, pepper, and nutmeg. Refrigerate until needed.

For the chips, using a swivel vegetable peeler, pare long thin strips off the pumpkin, then deep-fry in hot (300°F) vegetable oil, four or five strips at a time until golden and crisp. Drain on paper towels and set aside.

For the cappelletti, lay out the wonton wrappers on a flat surface, place $1/2$ tablespoon of filling in the center of each square. Brush the exterior of each square with a little water and fold over each square on the diagonal. Press the sides to seal. Hold one corner on the long side between thumb and index finger. Wrap around and press the two corners together. Place on a lightly floured tray and leave to dry for 30 minutes.

For the curried carrot cream, cook the diced carrot in the vegetable broth with the curry paste for 10 minutes. Transfer to a food processor and blend to a purée. Return to the pan, add the cream and butter, and bring to a boil. Season to taste, add some cilantro and keep warm.

Cook the cappelletti in a large pan of boiling salted water for 3–4 minutes, then remove, and drain well. Season and then toss with the curried carrot cream. Place on four serving plates, top with the pumpkin chips, and serve.

Green pea ravioli

with saffron butter and truffled beet salad

Fresh peas are obviously a lot more work for the preparation of these
ravioli, but really do make a difference. This dish always makes an
appearance on my menu when the first peas come into season in spring.

for the green pea ravioli

2 cups fresh shelled peas (or frozen)

1 tablespoon fresh mint leaves

3 1/2 ounces good quality ricotta cheese, well drained

2 green onions, finely chopped

1 tablespoon freshly squeezed lemon juice

1 recipe pasta dough (see PG TIPS page 112)

salt and freshly ground black pepper

for the saffron butter sauce

3/4 cup good vegetable broth

1/2 cup water from the cooking peas

1/2 cup heavy cream

good pinch of good quality saffron

* (or 1/2 teaspoon powdered)*

1/3 stick unsalted butter, chilled and cut into small pieces

salt and freshly ground black pepper

for the truffled beet salad

1 tablespoon balsamic vinegar

pinch of sugar

1/2 tablespoon truffle oil

1 medium-size beet, cooked, peeled, and cut into

* julienne strips (see PG TIPS)*

1 truffle, cut into julienne strips (optional)

3 tablespoons pea shoots

serves 6–8

For the ravioli, cook the peas in just enough boiling water to cover them for 5–6
minutes until tender and then drain (reserving 1/2 cup of the cooking water). Refresh
in iced water, drain again, and dry them well. Place in a food processor with the mint,
ricotta, and green onions and blend to a coarse purée. Remove to a bowl, season to
taste, and add the lemon juice.

Roll out the pasta into thin sheets, then brush a sheet with water and place
tablespoons of the pea-ricotta mixture on it, about 2 inches apart, in rows. Cover with
a second sheet of pasta, press down gently around the fillings, then cut the pasta into
squares with a fluted or plain pasta wheel or sharp knife. Check to ensure the edges
are well sealed, place on a lightly floured tray and leave to dry for 20 minutes.

For the saffron butter, heat the vegetable broth, reserved pea cooking liquid,
cream, and saffron in a pan and simmer until the liquid has reduced by half. Remove
from the heat, whisk in the chilled butter, season to taste, and then strain through a
fine strainer.

Cook the ravioli in plenty of simmering salted water for 3–4 minutes until al
dente, then remove with a slotted spoon, and drain well.

For the salad, whisk together the vinegar, sugar, and oil, add the beet and fresh
truffle, and adjust the seasoning; mix well.

Divide the ravioli among four serving dishes, pour over the saffron sauce, top with
the beet salad and pea shoots, and serve immediately.

PG TIPS   To cut the beet into julienne strips, simply cut the beet into 1/8 inch thick
slices on a kitchen mandolin or with a knife. Stack three or four of the slices on top of
each other, then slice them again, 1/8 inch thick.

Porcini pappardelle
with grilled figs

Dried porcini have a wonderful robust quality about their flavor. Here they make the base for a delicate wild mushroom pasta, which you will enjoy making again and again.

for the porcini pappardelle

1 ounce dried porcini mushrooms

2 garlic cloves, crushed

3 tablespoons extra-virgin olive oil

4 1/2 cups "00" pasta flour

3 free-range eggs

3 tablespoons olive oil

1 1/4 cups fresh porcini (or 2 ounces soaked and dried)

1 small mild red chili, deseeded and finely chopped

6 firm but ripe purple figs, cut into wedges

1/2 teaspoon caster sugar

2 tablespoons balsamic vinegar

3 tablespoons freshly grated castelli vegetalia
   (parmesan-style cheese)

juice of 1/2 lemon

salt, freshly ground black pepper, and ground nutmeg

serves 6–8

For the pasta, soak the porcini mushrooms in warm water for 20 minutes, reserving the soaking liquid. Rinse the mushrooms well and chop very finely. Mix with the garlic and oil. Sift the flour into a bowl. Make a well in the center, add the mushroom mixture and eggs, draw in the flour and gradually mix together to form a pliable dough. Knead for 10–12 minutes until smooth and elastic. Wrap the dough in plastic wrap and leave to rest for 1 hour. Divide the dough into four, then, working one piece at a time, roll it out until paper thin. Sprinkle with a little flour, then roll up. With a sharp knife, cut the roll widthwise into 1 inch wide ribbons. Unroll the ribbons and lay out on a lightly floured tray. Leave to dry for 30 minutes.

Preheat a broiler to its highest setting. Heat a skillet with 1 1/2 tablespoons of olive oil, add the fresh porcini and chili and cook over a high heat until the mushrooms are cooked and golden. Dust the figs with a little sugar, place on a cookie sheet, place under the grill and cook until lightly caramelized. (Alternatively this can be done in a small skillet.)

Put the reserved mushroom soaking liquid and 6 cups water in a large pan and bring to a boil. Cook the pasta for 3 minutes, or until al dente and drain well. Add the pasta to the mushrooms, stir in the vinegar, and fold in the parmesan. Toss together, add the lemon juice, and season with salt, pepper, and nutmeg and arrange on serving plates. Top with caramelized fig wedges and drizzle over the remaining olive oil and serve.

Spaghetti cacio e pepe

For this dish you will need to buy a chitarra or spaghetti guillotine,
available from good cooking stores or you can use the flat thinnest cutter
of a pasta roller. If not, substitute with good quality bought spaghetti.

1 recipe pasta dough (see PG TIPS page 112) or
  7 ounces dried spaghetti
1 tablespoon fresh black peppercorns
1 teaspoon pink peppercorns, rinsed
1 1/3 cups freshly grated pecorino romano cheese
salt

Prepare the dough in the normal manner but rest for 30 minutes. Divide the dough into four and roll out each piece through the thinnest cutters of a pasta roller. Cut the rolled pasta to fit the chitarra and trim the edges neatly. Using a rolling pin, roll out the pasta through the strings to create the spaghetti. Carefully remove the spaghetti and place on a lightly floured tray and leave to dry for 30 minutes. Lightly crush the black peppercorns in a mortar or coffee/spice grinder. Cook the spaghetti in a large pan of boiling salted water for 2–3 minutes or until al dente, then drain the pasta, reserving 3/4 cup cooking water. Heat a large skillet over a low heat, add half the crushed peppercorns and the pink peppercorns, and cook for 30 seconds, stirring constantly. Add the reserved cooking water and pecorino and heat for a further 30 seconds. Add the pasta, toss gently together, season with a little salt, and divide among four serving bowls. Sprinkle over the remaining black pepper and serve.

Saffron-cooked spaghetti
with baby spinach and fennel

Cooking the spaghetti in saffron water gives this dish an unbelievable
color as well as taste.

1 recipe pasta dough (see PG TIPS page 112) or
  7 ounces dried spaghetti
4 tablespoons extra-virgin olive oil
1 head of fennel, finely sliced, fronds removed
1 onion, thinly sliced
1/2 pound baby spinach leaves
5 tablespoons balsamic vinegar
2 good pinches of fresh saffron
2/3 cup pecorino romano cheese, grated
salt, freshly ground black pepper, and ground nutmeg

Make the spaghetti as above. Heat half the oil in a large frying pan. Add the fennel slices and onion and sauté over a moderate heat for 8–9 minutes or until soft and golden. Add the spinach and cook until it wilts, then add the balsamic vinegar.

Bring 4 cups water to a boil in a large pan, add the saffron, and leave to simmer for 5 minutes for the saffron to infuse the water. Cook the spaghetti in the saffron water for 2–3 minutes or until al dente. Drain well, reserving 1/2 cup cooking water. Add the reserved water to the vegetables and cook for 2–3 minutes. Add the cooked spaghetti, half the pecorino, toss well, and season with salt, freshly ground black pepper, and nutmeg. Place in four individual pasta bowls, top with the remaining pecorino, garnish with the reserved fennel fronds, and serve immediately.

Tagliatelle with caramelized witloof chicory
and deep-fried lemon zest

Either make your own pasta for this dish or buy one of the many fresh
varieties available in supermarkets—the quality is generally very good.

3 lemons

4 heads of witloof chicory (Belgian endive)

1/2 stick unsalted butter

1 teaspoon sugar

1/2 cup raisins, soaked in hot water for 30 minutes
*   and drained*

1/2 cup heavy cream

1 pound fresh or dried tagliatelle pasta

3 tablespoons freshly grated castelli vegetalia
*   (parmesan-style cheese)*

1/2 cup vegetable oil

salt and freshly ground black pepper

serves 6–8

Zest the lemons and place the zest into a small bowl. Halve the lemons and squeeze the juice over the zest, leave for 20 minutes to marinate and accentuate the flavor.

Remove and discard any tough or blemished outer leaves from the chicory. Trim a thin slice from the root ends, halve the chicory lengthwise and then shred crosswise into strips. Set aside. Melt the butter in a pan, add the chicory, sugar, a little salt and pepper, and sauté over a moderate heat for about 15 mintues, stirring occasionally, until the chicory is golden and caramelized. Add the raisins and cream. Remove the lemon zest, from the juices, dry them in a cloth, and add the juice to the chicory. Simmer for about 1–2 minutes until the sauce thickens. Keep warm.

Cook the tagliatelle in a large pan of boiling salted water for 2–3 minutes or until al dente, then drain, reserving 1/2 cup cooking water. Add the water to the lemon cream. Toss the sauce with the pasta and half the cheese and season to taste.

Heat the vegetable oil in a small pan and add the lemon zest and fry for about 1 minute until lightly golden and crisp. Drain on paper towels. Place the pasta into four individual serving bowls, sprinkle over the remaining cheese, and scatter over the crispy fried lemon. Serve immediately.

Tagliatelle with creamy brie
and semidry tomatoes

2 tablespoons unsalted butter

1 shallot, finely chopped

1/2 garlic clove, crushed

1 teaspoon fresh thyme leaves

1 cup semidry tomatoes in oil, drained

1 pound fresh or dried tagliatelle

1/2 cup crème fraîche or heavy cream

5 ounces brie, rind removed, sliced

salt and freshly ground black pepper

serves 6–8

Melt the butter in a pan, add the shallot and garlic, and cook over a low heat for 5 minutes. Add the thyme and tomatoes, increase the heat, and cook for about 2 minutes until softened. Cook the tagliatelle in boiling salted water until al dente and drain well. Add the crème fraîche and brie to the tomatoes and stir until melted. Return the pasta to the pan, pour over the sauce, and toss together. Season to taste and serve.

PG TIPS   Use a mixture of different tagliatelle, such as plain and spinach.

Fettucine with nettles
and garlic butter

Having fallen into many stinging nettles as a child, you can imagine my horror to find you used them in cooking! Perhaps it's our way of getting revenge. During the spring, nettles are at their best and most delicate. Ideally they should be no larger than the palm of your hand. Once picked, they lose their potency, and once cooked have no symptoms at all.

1 1/2 cups young stinging nettles, leaves only, plus
    12 leaves for the PG TIPS (pick them using sturdy gloves)

1 pound fresh or dried fettucine pasta

5 tablespoons unsalted butter

3 garlic cloves, crushed

1 teaspoon fennel seeds

3 tablespoons grated castelli vegetalia (parmesan-
    style cheese)

salt and freshly ground black pepper

serves 6–8

Chop the nettle leaves coarsely. Cook the fettucine in a large pan of boiling salted water until al dente. Drain and return to the pan. While the pasta is cooking, heat the butter in a heavy-based skillet over a low heat until the butter is foaming. Add the garlic and fennel seeds and cook for 30 seconds. Add the nettles and cook for a further 1 minute. Add the sauce to the pasta, scatter over the castelli vegetalia, and season. Toss well together and serve immediately.

PG TIPS   A nice idea is to top the pasta with some crispy deep-fried nettle leaves. Simply shallow-fry about twelves leaves in a pan of hot olive oil until crisp. Drain on paper towels.

Hot eggplant pasta
with black beans and peanut butter sauce

The Chinese black beans called for in this recipe are soy beans that have been fermented and salted.

1 pound fresh or dried penne pasta

4 tablespoons vegetable or sunflower oil

1 tablespoon sesame oil

1 eggplant, cut into 1/3 inch dice

1 inch piece of fresh ginger, peeled and finely chopped

1 garlic clove

2 tablespoons dried Chinese black beans, chopped

1 small green chili, deseeded and finely chopped

1 tablespoon sugar

2 tablespoons hoisin sauce

1 tablespoon smooth peanut butter

3 green onions, finely chopped

2 tablespoons chopped fresh cilantro

serves 6–8

Cook the penne in a large pan of boiling salted water until al dente and drain well. Heat both oils in a wok or large skillet, add the diced eggplant, ginger, and garlic, and stir-fry over a low heat for 2–3 minutes. Add the black beans and green chili and stir for a further 2 minutes. Add the sugar, hoisin sauce, and peanut butter and cook until reduced and thickened. Add the pasta to the sauce and then the green onions and cilantro. Stir until heated through and serve immediately.

Funghi carbonara

1 pound bucatini pasta (or spaghetti)

2 tablespoons unsalted butter

1 ounce dried wild mushrooms, soaked for 1 hour in water

1 shallot, finely chopped

5 ounces heavy cream

2 free-range eggs, beaten

1 cup grated castelli vegetalia (parmesan-style cheese)

salt, freshly ground black pepper, and ground nutmeg

serves 6–8

Cook the spaghetti in a large pan of boiling salted water until al dente and drain well. Heat the butter in a large skillet, add the mushrooms and shallot, and sauté for 3–4 minutes until softened. Add the cream, bring to a boil, and cook for 2–3 minutes or until the sauce has thickened lightly. Add the pasta and stir in the beaten eggs and castelli vegetalia. Toss well together and season with salt, pepper, and nutmeg. Serve immediately.

Twice-baked macaroni and celeriac soufflé
with Swiss fondue

A dish to tempt the most jaded of vegetarian palates. This one derives
from the classic Roux brothers' recipe enjoyed by diners at Le Gavroche in
London for many years. The beauty of this recipe is that they can be
made in advance (or even frozen if desired). In my recipe, pasta and
celery root is added to the basic recipe. It's delicious served as a starter
or, doubled up, as a wonderful main dish.

1 1/4 cups celeriac, peeled and cut into large dice

1/2 pound macaroni pasta (or sedani pasta)

1/2 stick unsalted butter

5 tablespoons plain flour

2 1/2 cups milk

5 free-range egg yolks

5 ounces roquefort cheese, crumbled

6 free-range egg whites

2 1/2 cups heavy cream

2 cups finely grated Swiss cheese

salt, freshly ground black pepper, and ground nutmeg

4 x 1 1/2 inch x 3 inch diameter tartlet molds or
   soufflé dishes

Place the celeriac in a pan, cover with boiling water and simmer for about 18–20
minutes until tender. Drain well and mash until smooth.

Cook the macaroni in a large pan of boiling salted water until al dente. Refresh in
cold water and drain well in a colander. Season with salt, pepper, and nutmeg.

Preheat the oven to 400°F. Melt the butter in a heavy-based pan, add the flour
and cook over a low heat for 1 minute. Add the milk, whisking all the time to prevent
lumps and, when smooth, cook for a further 3–4 minutes. Remove from the heat
and allow to cool slightly before beating in the egg yolks; season to taste. Stir in the
roquefort and celeriac and keep warm.

Whisk the egg whites until firm but not stiff. Add one third of the whisked whites
to the celeriac mixture, then gently fold in the remaining egg whites. Finally fold in the
cooked pasta, then spoon into four well buttered tartlet molds or soufflé dishes. Place
them in the oven for 3 minutes only, until the top of the soufflé begins to turn
golden. Remove (and cool if you are making in advance) and turn out the soufflés
into individual gratin dishes.

Heat the cream over a moderate heat and stir in the Swiss cheese. Pour the
fondue over the soufflés, then return to the oven for a further 5 minutes before
serving immediately.

PG TIPS   For a little extra texture, you could top each soufflé with crisp cheese
cracknel (see page 38).

Naked spinach ravioli

with macaroni and vegetable arrabiata dressing

In this recipe the ravioli filling is detached from its pasta casing, which is served alongside in the form of macaroni. These are the lightest of spinach dumplings imaginable, topped with a deliciously spicy dressing.

1/2 pound fresh spinach, washed and stalks removed

3/4 cup good quality ricotta cheese, well drained

1 free-range egg

3 cups plain flour

3 tablespoons freshly grated castelli vegetalia
  (parmesan-style cheese)

1/2 pound macaroni pasta (1/2 inch thick)

salt, freshly ground black pepper, and nutmeg

for the vegetable arrabiata dressing

1/2 cup olive oil

2 shallots, finely chopped

2 garlic cloves, crushed

2 small dried red chilies, finely chopped

1 large zucchini, finely diced

6 tomatoes, blanched, skinned, deseeded, and chopped

2 tablespoons pitted, chopped black olives

juice of 1/2 lemon

3 tablespoons chopped fresh cilantro

salt and freshly ground black pepper

Cook the spinach in a heated skillet until wilted in its own juices. Transfer to a colander and squeeze out any excess liquid. Place in a blender and blend to a purée. Transfer to a bowl. Add the ricotta, egg, flour, and parmesan, season with salt, pepper, and nutmeg and stir. (If it's too dry, add 2 tablespoons of cold water.) Cover with plastic wrap and refrigerate for 1 hour.

For the dressing, heat the olive oil in a pan, add the shallots, garlic, and chilies and cook over a moderate heat for 30 seconds. Raise the heat, add the zucchini and fry for 2 minutes. Add the tomatoes and olives and cook for a further 2–3 minutes. Add the lemon juice and cilantro and season to taste. Keep warm.

To make the dumplings, use floured hands to roll the spinach mix into small 1/2 inch balls. Bring a large pan of salted water to a boil, then carefully drop the dumplings into the water. When they rise to the surface (after a few minutes), remove them with a slotted spoon and drain well. Meanwhile, cook the macaroni in a large pan of boiling salted water until al dente. Toss the dumplings and pasta in the dressing, season to taste, and divide among four serving bowls. Serve immediately.

Main dishes

Most people judge a style or type of cooking on the strength of the main course. The recent movement of vegetarian cookery has been to lighten dishes, use more digestible textures, and include brighter and bolder seasonings inspired by cuisines from around the world. The care and preparation of main dishes make such a difference to the visual appeal of a meal and thus diner satisfaction. In this chapter, I hope you will enjoy my choice of varied dishes produced with seasonal prime vegetables.

Cauliflower and date tagine
with Tunisian pilaf

For many people dates are too sweet and should only be confined to sticky-based Middle Eastern-style pastries—not so! Within this north African cauliflower tagine they are wonderful, working in harmony with the delicate spices. Dates have been a staple food in desert lands for thousands of years.

1 large cauliflower, cut into florets

1 tablespoon plain flour

1/2 teaspoon chili powder

1 teaspoon ground coriander

1 teaspoon ground ginger

good pinch of ground turmeric

4 tablespoons olive oil

1 onion, chopped

1 garlic clove, crushed

1 pound canned peeled tomatoes, chopped

1/2 cup pitted dates

3 cups good vegetable broth

3 tablespoons chopped fresh cilantro

2 tablespoons chopped fresh mint

salt and freshly ground black pepper

for the Tunisian pilaff

2 tablespoons olive oil

1/4 cup whole blanched almonds

1 onion, chopped

1/4 cup currants

1 teaspoon ground cinnamon

13/4 cups long-grain rice

3 cups good vegetable broth, hot

zest of 1 orange

Blanch the cauliflower florets in boiling water for 1 minute, drain, refresh under cold running water, and dry in a cloth. Place in a bowl with the flour and spices and leave for 2 hours to allow the flavors to infuse.

Heat the oil in a heavy-based pan, add the cauliflower and spices, and fry lightly together over a low heat for 5 minutes until golden on all sides. Add the onion and garlic and cook for a further 2 minutes. Add the tomatoes, dates, and vegetable broth and simmer for 15–20 minutes. Finally stir in the herbs and season to taste.

Meanwhile, for the pilaf, heat the oil in a pan, add the almonds, and cook for 5–6 minutes until golden. Remove them, add the onion and currants to the oil, and cook for 2 minutes. Add the cinnamon and cook for a further 30 seconds. Add the rice and coat with the onions and cinnamon. Pour over the hot stock, cover, and cook over a low heat for 15 minutes. Remove from the heat and leave, covered, for a further 5 minutes. Stir in the orange zest and almonds, adjust the seasoning, and serve alongside the tagine.

Swiss chard and corn crespelle
with chèvre

Crespelle is the Italian name for these delicate, yet simple, light pancakes flavored with corn, filled with a creamy chard and nut filling, and baked in the oven until slightly crispy. The pancakes can be made a day in advance, then kept wrapped in plastic wrap. To reheat, wrap them in foil and place in the oven at 375°F for 10–15 minutes.

1 1/2 cups all-purpose flour

2 free-range eggs

1/2 cup milk

2 cups canned corn, drained

1 tablespoon olive oil (plus some extra for cooking
  the pancakes)

1 red onion, chopped

3/4 pound Swiss chard, stalks discarded, chopped

2 tablespoons balsamic vinegar

1/2 pound chèvre

5 tablespoons pine nuts

2 tablespoons chopped fresh mint

salt and freshly ground black pepper

Sift the flour into a bowl, add the eggs and milk, and mix together. Place half the corn in a food processor, pour on the egg mixture, and blend to a batter. Chop the remaining corn. Transfer the batter to a bowl, add the chopped corn, and set aside for 30 minutes. The consistency should be that of light cream so add a little more milk if necessary.

Preheat the oven to 350°F. Heat the olive oil in a large skillet, add the onion, and sauté over a low heat until golden. Add the chopped chard and cook for 4–5 minutes. Pour over the vinegar, add half the chèvre, the pine nuts, and mint. Season to taste and keep warm.

Heat a little olive oil in a 6 inch nonstick skillet over a moderate heat. Fill a 1/4 cup ladle or large spoon with batter and pour into the pan, tilting it so that the batter covers the base. Cook until pale golden or until the mixture begins to bubble. Turn it over and cook on the other side. Continue the process until all the batter is used up. You will need twelve crespelle in total. Fill each crespelle with the chard mixture and fold in half, flattening it lightly. Place in a well buttered gratin dish (using about 1 tablespoon of butter). Smear over the remaining chèvre and place in the oven until golden and slightly crispy. Serve immediately.

Summer vegetables
with salsa all'agresto

The height of summer is the time to enjoy these twice-cooked vegetables. Salsa all'agresto is an Italian sauce which dates back to the Middle Ages. Similar in makeup to pesto, made with nuts, oil, and herbs, but with the addition of verjuice (or unripened grape juice), it provides an intriguing flavor that gives us a glimpse of what people ate hundreds of years ago. If you can't find verjuice, try a mix of white wine vinegar, lemon juice and a little sugar. Serve with crusty bread to mop up the juices.

4 tablespoons extra-virgin olive oil

4 small eggplants, halved

4 plum tomatoes, halved

2 large zucchini, cut into thick wedges

12 asparagus tips, peeled and trimmed

1 garlic clove, crushed

for the salsa all'agresto

$1/4$ cup almonds

2 garlic cloves, crushed

good pinch of sugar

6 tablespoons mixed herbs (flat-leaf parsley and basil)

$1/2$ cup olive oil

6 tablespoons verjuice

salt and freshly ground black pepper

Preheat the oven to 425°F. Heat a ridged skillet until hot and then brush all over with a little olive oil. Add the vegetables and fry for 6–8 minutes on each side until soft and slightly charred. Remove the vegetables and place in a well oiled gratin dish.

For the salsa all'agresto, place the almonds, garlic, sugar, and herbs in a food processor and blend until roughly chopped. With the motor running, add the oil in a thin stream through the funnel at the top, then do the same with the verjuice. Season. Spoon the salsa over the vegetables, cover the dish with foil, and bake for 5 minutes, then remove the foil and cook for a further 2–3 minutes until lightly golden.

PG TIPS For a lovely variation, mix in some buffalo mozzarella with the vegetables before covering with the salsa all'agresto.

Vegetable stifado
with spinach and tomato keftedes

A rich vegetable stew, based on a traditional Greek recipe made with morsels of beef. This vegetarian variety can be made in advance and reheated when needed. I recommend a large basket of crusty bread to mop up any remaining juices.

4 tablespoons olive oil

$^1/2$ pound button onions

2 garlic cloves, crushed

1 teaspoon ground cumin

1 medium-size cauliflower, cut into florets

2 large carrots, peeled and cut into thick slices

5 ounces new potatoes, peeled and halved

1 tablespoon all-purpose flour

$^3/4$ cup red wine

3 cups good vegetable broth

$^1/2$ cup semidry tomatoes in oil, drained

1 cup cooked navy beans

sprig of rosemary

12 black olives

2 tablespoons chopped fresh flat-leaf parsley

1 teaspoon chopped fresh oregano

salt and freshly ground black pepper

for the keftedes

4 ripe plum tomatoes, deseeded and chopped

$^1/4$ cup cooked spinach, chopped

2 green onions, finely chopped

$^1/2$ teaspoon sugar

3 tablespoons self-rising flour

olive oil

salt and freshly ground black pepper

Preheat the oven to 375°F. Heat half the oil in an ovenproof casserole over a moderate heat, add the button onions, and cook for about 4–5 minutes until lightly golden. Add the garlic and cook for a further 1 minute. Add the cumin, cauliflower florets, carrots, and potatoes and toss well together. Add the flour, stir well, and cook for a further 1 minute. Add the red wine and broth, bring to a boil, and add the tomatoes, cooked beans, and rosemary. Place in the oven for 35–45 minutes until tender. When cooked, remove from the oven and stir in the remaining olive oil, then add the olives, parsley, and oregano. Adjust the seasoning and keep hot (or cool if reheating later).

For the keftedes, place the tomatoes, spinach, green onions, and sugar in a bowl and season to taste. Add flour until the mixture is thick but still moist. Heat a little olive oil in a large nonstick skillet and, when hot, drop spoonfuls of the tomato and spinach mixture into the oil, then fry on both sides for 2–3 minutes until golden. Drain on paper towels to remove excess grease and serve alongside the stifado.

Baked open cap mushrooms
with paneer and cumin spinach

The rise of Indian food over the last five years has been amazing, with
good quality, highly rated restaurants springing up all over the place.
Here is a dish using paneer, an Indian curd cheese, now available from
leading stores and Indian delicatessens.

8 large open cap mushrooms

4 tablespoons vegetable oil

6 ounces paneer cheese, cut into 1/2 inch dice

1/2 teaspoon coriander seeds

1/3 inch piece of fresh ginger, peeled and finely chopped

1 small onion, finely chopped

1 small green chili, deseeded and chopped

6 firm but ripe tomatoes

1 teaspoon tomato paste

pinch of saffron

1/2 teaspoon chili powder

1 teaspoon fenugreek seeds

1 teaspoon garam masala

1 tablespoon honey

3 tablespoons chopped fresh cilantro

for the cumin spinach

1/2 teaspoon cumin seeds

1 garlic clove, crushed

1 pound fresh spinach, washed

salt and freshly ground black pepper

2 cups cooked basmati rice

Preheat the oven to 350°F. Remove and roughly dice the stems of the mushrooms. Heat 3 tablespoons of oil in a large skillet, add the mushrooms, and cook for 3–4 minutes until golden. Remove and leave to cool. Add the paneer in two batches to the oil, fry until brown all over, and set aside.

Heat the remaining oil in another skillet and add the mushroom stems and cook for 2–3 minutes. Add the coriander seeds, ginger, onion, and chili and cook for 3–4 minutes or until softened and golden. Add the tomatoes, tomato paste, and saffron and cook for a further 5 minutes. Add the remaining spices and honey. Transfer the paneer and half the cilantro to the sauce.

Place the mushrooms in the base of a lightly greased ovenproof or baking dish. Fill each mushroom with the paneer mixture, then transfer the dish to the oven to bake for 6–8 minutes.

For the spinach, heat a skillet over a moderate heat, add the cumin seeds and dry-fry for 30 seconds. Add the garlic and washed spinach and cook over a high heat until the spinach has wilted and any water evaporated. Season to taste.

Serve the stuffed baked mushrooms with the spinach and some basmati rice, sprinkle over the remaining cilantro, and serve.

Saag kebobs
with tomato and banana pickle and coconut yogurt

Throughout the subcontinent different religions impose food taboos that are rigidly adhered to. Many Indians are strict vegetarians, enjoying a cuisine that is in a class of its own and could convert even the most dedicated meat lover. These Indian-style spinach (saag) fritters are delicious. Make them smaller in size to serve as an appetizer.

for the tomato and banana pickle

2 tablespoons vegetable oil

1 teaspoon ground cumin

1 teaspoon ground cardamom

1 tablespoon mustard seeds

3 garlic cloves, crushed

1 teaspoon ground turmeric

$1/2$ teaspoon cayenne pepper

1 pound ripe but firm tomatoes, chopped

2 tablespoons malt vinegar

1 tablespoon superfine sugar

2 bananas, peeled and cut into small dice

1 inch piece of fresh ginger, peeled and grated

for the coconut yogurt

$1/2$ cup natural yogurt

3 tablespoons freshly grated coconut (or desiccated is fine)

2 tablespoons chopped fresh mint

for the spinach fritters

$1/2$ cup semolina

$1/4$ pound fresh spinach, picked and chopped

1 green chili, deseeded

3 tablespoons cumin seeds, lightly toasted

good pinch of bicarbonate soda

1 tablespoon lemon juice

vegetable oil for deep-frying

small fresh mint leaves

salt and freshly ground black pepper

Prepare the pickle a day or two in advance. Heat the oil in a pan and add the cumin, cardamom, mustard seeds, and garlic. Cook over a low heat until the garlic starts to brown. Add the turmeric, cayenne, and chopped tomatoes, stir, and cook for 2 minutes. Add the vinegar, sugar, bananas, and ginger and simmer for about 10–15 minutes until thickened. Leave to cool then refrigerate, covered, until needed.

For the coconut yogurt, simply mix the ingredients together.

For the fritters, blend all the ingredients (except the oil and mint) in a food processor with approximately $1/3$ cup cold water to form a thick batter, then leave to stand for 30 minutes before use.

Heat the vegetable oil to 325°F. When ready, drop tablespoonfuls of the mixture into the hot oil and deep-fry for 1–2 minutes until crisp and golden. Remove with a slotted spoon and place on paper towels to drain.

Place equal amounts of fritters on four serving plates with some tomato and banana pickle, drizzle with a little yogurt, and serve some separately on the side. Scatter over the mint leaves and serve.

Kerala pumpkin curry
with cinnamon rice and beet raita

Curry leaves are small shiny flat leaves very similar in appearance to bay
leaves. They are delicate and wonderfully flavored, and can be found in
Indian stores—well worth sourcing. The beet-flavored raita makes not only
a wonderful accompaniment, but finishes off a stunningly colorful dish.

2 tablespoons sunflower oil

1 large onion, chopped

2 inch piece of fresh ginger, peeled and chopped

3 garlic cloves, crushed

$^1/2$ teaspoon cumin seeds, lightly crushed

1 teaspoon good turmeric

$^1/2$ teaspoon chili powder

1 pound pumpkin, peeled, deseeded and cut
    into large pieces

$^3/4$ cup coconut milk

1 teaspoon mustard seeds

2 green chilies, chopped

8 curry leaves

$^3/4$ cup yogurt

for the beet raita

$^1/2$ cup natural yogurt

$^1/2$ teaspoon salt

$^1/2$ teaspoon sugar

pinch of ground cumin

2 medium-size beets, cooked (see page 77), peeled,
    and cut into 1cm dice

2 tablespoons chopped fresh mint

2 cups basmati rice, scented with cinnamon
    (see PG TIPS)

Heat half the oil in a heavy-based pan, add the onion, and cook over a low heat for
8–10 minutes until soft. Meanwhile, blend the ginger and garlic to a paste together in
a small food processor (or a pestle and mortar if you prefer). Add the paste to the
onion and cook for 2–3 minutes. Add the cumin seeds, turmeric, and chili powder
and cook for a further 1 minute. Throw in the pumpkin, mix well with the spices, add
the coconut milk, and simmer for about 15 minutes until cooked. (Do not let the
pumpkin cook too much or it will go mushy.)

For the raita, place the yogurt in a bowl, add the salt, sugar, and cumin, stir in the
beets and chopped mint.

Heat a small skillet with the remaining oil, throw in the mustard seeds, chilies,
and curry leaves and cook for 30 seconds until the seeds begin to pop. Add to the
pumpkin curry along with the yogurt and heat through for 2 minutes. Serve with the
cinnamon-scented rice and beet raita.

PG TIPS   For a fragrant sweet-tasting rice to accompany the curry, simply cook the
rice as normal, but with the addition of some broken cinnamon sticks in with the
water. Remove before serving.

Black bean piperade
with melted cheddar and mint mojo verde

This is a great brunch or substantial lunch dish. A piperade is an egg dish flavored with ratatouille-style vegetables, a speciality of southern France. In this recipe, I take the dish to Mexico for a spicier variation on the theme with a Cuban mojo salsa. Both the vegetables and the spicy green mojo sauce are all the better made in advance, allowing their flavors to develop. I suggest some country-style bread to serve with the piperades.

for the mint mojo verde

2 garlic cloves, peeled

1 1/2 tablespoons fresh cilantro leaves

2 tablespoons fresh mint leaves

1 green bell pepper, deseeded and chopped

1 small green chili, chopped

1/2 cup fresh white breadcrumbs

3 tablespoons olive oil

1 tablespoon white wine vinegar

4 tablespoons olive oil

1 onion, finely chopped

1 garlic clove, crushed

1 green chili, deseeded and finely chopped

1/2 yellow bell pepper, deseeded and cut into 1/3 inch dice

1/2 red bell pepper, deseeded and cut into 1/3 inch dice

1 zucchini, cut into 1/3 inch dice

1/2 cup cooked Mexican black beans (canned are fine)

1 tablespoon tomato paste

8 free-range eggs, separated

olive oil

2/3 cup freshly grated vegetarian cheddar cheese

salt and freshly ground black pepper

For the mint mojo verde, place the garlic, cilantro, mint, pepper, and green chili in a small food processor and blend until finely chopped. Add the breadcrumbs, oil and vinegar, and blend again, scraping down the sides to ensure it is thoroughly mixed—the mojo should be a thick sauce. Set aside.

Heat half the olive oil in a large skillet, add the onion, garlic, and chili and cook over a moderate heat until softened and tender. Add all the vegetables and the beans and cook for 2–3 minutes. Add the tomato paste and 2 tablespoons of water and mix well with the vegetables. Lower the heat, cover the pan with a lid, and cook for 10–15 minutes until the vegetables are tender. Season to taste and leave to cool. Refrigerate if making in advance.

To make the piperade, whisk the egg whites until stiff, then add to the yolks. Incorporate together and season.

Divide the vegetables into four equal amounts and the egg mixture also into four amounts. Heat each portion of vegetables in a little olive oil in a nonstick omelette pan or small skillet. When hot, add the egg mixture and stir well together. Cook over a low heat until the piperade has a mousse-like consistency. Slide out the piperade onto a serving plate or shallow bowl, top with some of the cheddar, and spoon on the mint mojo sauce. Cook one or two at at a time and keep warm while preparing the rest in the same way.

Vegetarian pho

Another delectable, Asian-style, heart-warming broth, this time from Vietnam. Traditionally made with meat and fish, this vegetarian version is seasoned with vegetarian fish sauce—don't fear, this one is only made of chilies, water, leeks, vinegar, and sugar. You should ask for it at your oriental grocers. A smaller version can be served as an appetizer.

for the base broth

8 1/2 cups good vegetable broth

2 tablespoons soy sauce

6 garlic cloves, crushed

1 onion, chopped

1 inch piece of fresh ginger, peeled and grated

1 stick of cinnamon

2 star anise

1 bay leaf

2 stalks of celery, thinly sliced

4 spring onions, finely shredded

2 carrots, finely shredded

1/2 pound Chinese cabbage, finely shredded

3/4 cup beansprouts

1 teaspoon vegetarian fish sauce (nuoc mam chay)

2 tablespoons soy sauce

12 ounces buckwheat soba noodles

20 fresh basil leaves

6 tablespoons fresh cilantro

1 red chili, thinly sliced

1 lime, cut into wedges

salt and freshly ground black pepper

For the broth, place the broth, soy sauce, garlic, and onion in a pan and bring to a boil. Add the ginger, cinnamon stick, star anise, and bay leaf. Reduce the heat to a simmer and cook for 20 minutes. Strain the broth and replace on the heat.

Add all the vegetables, vegetarian fish sauce, and soy sauce and cook for 10 minutes. Add the noodles and simmer for a further 5 minutes. Season. Pour into four large serving bowls, top with the herbs and chili, squeeze over the lime juice, and serve.

Funghi and grilled vegetable moussaka
with red ricotta glaze

Moussaka is a staple served in tavernas and prepared in homes throughout Greece. The wild mushrooms add a touch of elegance and the grilled vegetables a light smoky flavor that works so well when paired together. A fresh well dressed green salad makes a great accompaniment.

1 pound potatoes, peeled and cut into $^1/_3$ inch thick slices

3 eggplants, cut into $^1/_3$ inch thick slices

3 red bell peppers, halved, deseeded, and cut into large pieces

2 zucchini, cut into $^1/_3$ inch thick slices

2 tablespoons extra-virgin olive oil

1 onion, finely chopped

2 garlic cloves, crushed

2 tablespoons chopped fresh oregano

1 ounce dried wild mushrooms, soaked in a little red wine and drained

$^1/_4$ cup raisins

1 pound canned plum tomatoes, drained

1 tablespoon tomato paste

salt and freshly ground black pepper

for the red ricotta glaze
2 free-range egg yolks

1 garlic clove, crushed

$2^1/_2$ cups passata

$^2/_3$ cup ricotta cheese

$^1/_2$ cup heavy cream

salt and freshly ground black pepper

$1^3/_4$ pint ovenproof casserole dish

Heat a ridged skillet and, when smoking, brush the potatoes, eggplant, peppers, and zucchini with a little olive oil, then cook for 8–10 minutes until tender and lightly charred all over. Season well and set aside.

Heat the remaining olive oil in a pan, add the onion, garlic, oregano, mushrooms, and raisins and cook over a moderate heat for 4–5 minutes before adding the chopped tomatoes and tomato paste. Cook for 10–15 minutes until the sauce becomes thick with very little sauce left.

Preheat the oven to 325°F. Lightly grease the casserole dish. Pour the wild mushroom sauce into the base of the dish, then arrange overlapping slices of the grilled vegetables over the surface, with an eye for color.

For the glaze, beat the egg yolks, garlic, passata, and ricotta in a bowl. Pour in the cream and season well. Pour the egg mixture over the vegetables, making sure all the vegetables are covered. Place in the oven to bake for 20 minutes, or until the top is golden brown. Remove from the oven and allow to sit for 2–3 minutes before cutting into portions to serve.

Green jungle curry
with lychees, green bell peppers, and coconut rice cakes

Unlike most versions that generally contain coconut milk, this Thai curry is
thin in appearance, full of vegetables, and quite spicy. Originally jungle
curries were made of wild boar, but nowadays they are more likely to be
made with chicken or pork. This vegetarian version is wonderful.

for the rice cakes

1 cup coconut milk

1 teaspoon ground turmeric

1 cup Thai jasmine rice

1 free-range egg yolk

2 tablespoons unsalted butter

2 tablespoons vegetable oil

2 shallots, thinly sliced

1 inch piece of fresh ginger, peeled and finely chopped

*2 stalks of lemongrass, outer casing discarded,
   finely chopped*

1/2 teaspoon fennel seeds, crushed

1 heaped tablespoon Thai green curry paste

1/2 pound sugar snap peas

5 ounces baby corn

1/4 pound French string beans, trimmed

1 large turnip, peeled and cut into 1/2 inch dice

8 ounces Thai pea aubergines

8 asparagus tips

4 cups good vegetable broth

10 Thai basil leaves

4 kaffir lime leaves, shredded

1 teaspoon green peppercorns

1 small can lychees, drained

8 inch x 12 inch baking/cake pan

For the rice cakes, put 1 cup water, the coconut milk, and turmeric in a pan and bring
to a boil. Add the rice and simmer gently for 10–15 minutes until cooked and all the
liquid has gone. Mix in the egg yolk, then remove to a greased baking pan or cake
pan, spread over with a palette knife to ensure the top is smooth. Refrigerate to
set overnight.

For the curry, heat the oil in a pan, add the shallots, ginger, lemongrass, and
fennel seeds and cook for 1 minute. Add the Thai curry paste and stir together to
infuse the flavors. Add the vegetables, toss with the spices, then add the vegetable
broth and bring to a boil. Add the Thai basil, kaffir lime leaves, and peppercorns and
reduce to a simmer. Cook gently for 10–12 minutes or until the vegetables are
tender. Add the lychees and heat through.

Take the rice from the fridge, remove from the pan and cut the slab into neat
2 inch square cakes. Fry in the butter for 1–2 minutes on each side until crisp.

Serve the curry into four serving bowls and garnish each with a small pile of fried
coconut rice cakes.

Eggplant and mozzarella croquettes
with sherry-glazed vegetables

The use of Japanese-style breadcrumbs called panko to coat the eggplant rolls gives this dish a real crispiness when fried. By adding honey to them, they obtain a wonderful golden color, an idea I learnt from a great chef and friend, Peter Gordon. Panko are available from oriental stores, although fresh white breadcrumbs can be used instead. I often serve this dish with garlic mayonnaise (aïoli—see PG TIPS page 102) to be passed around the table.

2 medium-size eggplants, stalks removed

1/2 cup olive oil

6 ounces mozzarella, thinly sliced

1/2 cup semidry tomatoes, drained and chopped

3 tablespoons all-purpose flour

2 free-range eggs, lightly beaten

1 cup panko crumbs (mixed with 2 tablespoons honey)

vegetable oil for deep-frying

for the vegetables

2 red bell peppers, deseeded and cut into thick strips

2 yellow bell peppers, deseeded and cut into thick strips

1 red onion, cut into large dice

2 garlic cloves, halved

2 ounces black olives

4 small baby zucchini, cut into slices on bias

1 teaspoon light brown sugar

1/2 cup dry sherry

4 sprigs of rosemary

3 tablespoons olive oil

salt and freshly ground black pepper

toothpicks

Preheat the oven to 400°F. Using a large knife, cut the eggplants lengthwise into 1/3 inch thick slices. Heat the olive oil in a large skillet. When hot add the eggplant slices a few at a time and cook for 2–3 minutes on each side until golden. Remove with a slotted spoon onto paper towels to drain and cool.

Place twelve cooked slices onto a work surface, divide the mozzarella and top the eggplant with it. Place a spoonful of chopped tomatoes on top and carefully roll them up tightly. Secure with a toothpick, then dust all over with flour. Dip in the beaten egg, then coat in the honey-coated panko crumbs. Brush off any excess crumbs, place on a plate, and refrigerate.

For the vegetables, place the peppers, onion, garlic, olives, and zucchini in a large roasting pan. Sprinkle over the sugar, pour over the sherry, and season with a little salt and pepper. Cover the pan with foil and bake for 40 minutes. Remove the foil, add the rosemary and olive oil, and return to the oven, uncovered, for a further 10 minutes until the vegetables are tender.

Meanwhile, heat the vegetable oil in a skillet or large pan. When hot (approximately 325°F), carefully immerse half the eggplant croquettes and cook for about 2–3 minutes until golden and crisp. Remove with a slotted spoon and drain on paper towels. Cook the remainder in the same way. Arrange the croquettes on a bed of the sherry-glazed vegetables on four serving plates and serve.

PG TIPS   These sherry-glazed vegetables are wonderful served just on their own, topped with grated feta and crispy bread, as an appetizer.

Bombay tortillas

with spiced squash, peas, and coconut yogurt

A real East-meets-West dish here. Mexican flour tortillas—a staple of Mexican eating—form a wrap for a spiced squash and pea filling and are then baked under a thin veil of yogurt and mild cheese.

2 tablespoons ghee or unsalted butter

1 onion, chopped

1 poblano chili, roasted (see PG TIPS)

12 ounces butternut squash or pumpkin, peeled and cut into 1 inch dice

8 ounces canned plum tomatoes, chopped

1/2 cup semidry tomatoes

1 teaspoon cumin seeds

1/2 teaspoon ground coriander

2/3 cup fresh or frozen peas

8 flour tortillas

2 tablespoons chopped fresh cilantro

coconut yogurt (see page 135)

1 cup freshly grated vegetarian mild cheddar cheese

Preheat the oven to 400°F. In a large skillet, heat the ghee or butter, add the onion and cook for 2–3 minutes. Shred the roasted poblano chili, add to the pan, and cook for a further 2 minutes. Add the squash and cook for 15–20 minutes over a moderate heat. Add both types of tomato, cumin seeds, ground coriander, and peas, then reduce the heat and cook for 5 minutes to infuse the flavors and form a sauce.

Lay out the flour tortillas on a work surface, fill with the squash mixture, then roll them up tightly to secure the filling. Place them in a large well buttered (using about 1 tablespoon of butter) ovenproof gratin dish, then spoon over the yogurt and sprinkle with chopped cilantro. Liberally scatter over the cheese, then transfer to the oven to heat through for about 8–10 minutes before serving.

PG TIPS   Roasting chilies like the Mexicans do really brings out their flavor. To roast them, simply place them directly over a gas flame and leave for 2–3 minutes, turning them occasionally until blistered and black in color. Alternatively place under a hot preheated broiler until charred, turning them regularly. When charred, place in a small plastic kitchen bag and seal it tightly to allow the chilies to steam for 5 minutes and loosen their skins. Peel off their skins, half them, then remove the inner seeds and use as required.

Bubble and squeak frittata

with crumbled feta and olives

For this dish be sure to use good firm waxy potatoes, like Charlottes or Juliettes, which are not only great tasting, but hold their shape during cooking too. This is a great lunch dish served with a simple salad or for a hearty brunch or breakfast treat. Make this recipe as one large dish or four smaller individual ones.

1 pound waxy potatoes, peeled and cut into
 small ¹/3 inch dice

1²/3 cups chopped savoy cabbage

12 free-range eggs

³/4 cup milk

1 teaspoon chopped fresh rosemary (plus a little
 for garnishing)

2 tablespoons unsalted butter

2 tablespoons olive oil

¹/2 garlic clove, crushed

¹/4 pound Greek feta cheese, crumbled

12 black olives, pitted and roughly chopped

salt and freshly ground black pepper

Preheat the oven to 350°F. Cook the potatoes and cabbage in separate pans of boiling water for 20–25 minutes until just cooked, then drain them well and dry them both.

Beat the eggs and milk in a bowl with the rosemary and a little salt and pepper.

Place a heavy-based skillet over a moderate heat and add the butter and olive oil. Add the cooked potatoes, cabbage and the garlic, stir together well in the oil and butter, and cook for 6–8 minutes. Pour over the egg mixture and cook until it begins to set at the edges. Using a fork, draw the edges into the middle, allowing the edges to set again. Sprinkle over the feta and olives, transfer to the oven, and cook for 7–10 minutes or until firm. Slide onto a plate, garnish with rosemary, and serve.

Baked bell peppers

with chickpea and apricot pilau and smoked almond dukkah

An excellent dish packed full of energy and flavor with its roots in the Middle East. The use of smoked almonds for the dukkah—a spiced seasoning popular in Egypt—adds a wonderful smoky overtone to the dish. I suggest serving the peppers on a bed of buttered garlic spinach and roasted squash.

1 1/2 cups good vegetable broth

good pinch of saffron

1 1/3 cups brown rice

6 tablespoons olive oil

3 tablespoons pine nuts

1 onion, finely chopped

1/2 teaspoon ground coriander

1/2 teaspoon ground cumin

3/4 cup cooked chickpeas (canned are fine), drained

1/4 cup raisins

1/4 cup dried apricots, soaked in water, drained and chopped

1 tablespoon flat-leaf parsley, chopped

4 large red bell peppers, halved and deseeded, stalks intact

4 tablespoons balsamic vinegar

2 tablespoons honey

salt and freshly ground black pepper

smoked almond dukkah

1/4 cup smoked almonds

1 tablespoon sesame seeds

1 tablespoon coriander seeds

1/2 teaspoon cumin seeds

little salt and freshly cracked black pepper

Preheat the oven to 400°F. Gently heat the vegetable broth in a pan and infuse the saffron in it for 4–5 minutes. Add the rice and simmer, covered, for 20–25 minutes or until the rice is tender and all the broth has been absorbed.

Heat 3 tablespoons of the oil in a large nonstick skillet, add the pine nuts, and cook over a low heat until golden; remove and set aside. Heat the remaining 3 tablespoons of oil in the pan, add the onion, and cook until lightly golden. Add the ground coriander, cumin, chickpeas, raisins, and apricots and cook for 1 minute. Stir in the rice, add the chopped parsley, and season to taste. Fill the pepper halves with the prepared pilau and place in a large roasting pan. Mix together the vinegar, honey, and 1/2 cup water, then pour the liquid into the base of the roasting pan. Place the pan in the oven and cook for 35–40 minutes.

For the smoked almond dukkah, heat a dry skillet and, when hot, add the almonds and seeds and toast for 30 seconds, stirring all the time. Transfer to a mortar and crush with a pestle, but not too finely, and season.

When the peppers are cooked, remove to four serving plates, sprinkle liberally with the dukkah, whisk the pan cooking juices, and pour over the peppers.

PG TIPS The dukkah can be made in advance and kept in a sealed container. It is great sprinkled on salads and over fried eggs. It is also becoming increasingly popular as a dry-spice dip for olive oil-drenched slices of bread in restaurants.

Butternut squash and blue cheese tacos
with white truffle oil

The slightly sweet-tasting squash is complemented here by the sharp blue cheese, making an interesting combination. White truffle oil is becoming a more common ingredient now, since it gives a good perfume to foods, but at a fraction of the cost of fresh truffles. A ridged skillet will do fine, but for the best results use a charcoal grill.

4 tablespoons olive oil (plus more for coating)

3/4 pound butternut squash (or other winter squash), peeled and cut into 1/2 inch dice

1 garlic clove, crushed

2/3 cup canned corn, well drained

1 small onion, finely chopped

1/4 pound roquefort (or other blue cheese)

1 teaspoon fresh thyme leaves

4 x 6 inch corn tortillas

2 tablespoons white truffle oil

salt and freshly ground black pepper

Heat the olive oil in a large skillet over a moderate heat, add the squash, garlic, corn, and onion and cook for 8–10 minutes until golden and just tender when pierced with a knife. Remove to a bowl, add the roquefort and thyme, and lightly mash with a fork. Season to taste and leave to cool.

Place the tortillas on a flat surface, fill the center of each with the cheese mixture, then fold each tortilla in half over the filling to make a semicircle. Brush the tops lightly with olive oil. Place on a preheated charcoal grill or ridged skillet and cook for about 2–3 minutes until golden brown. Brush with olive oil, turn over, and cook on the other side. Drizzle with the truffle oil and serve.

Persian ratatouille-baked tomatoes

with cashew kibbeh crust

Stuffed vegetables are popular all over the Middle East and date back to ancient times. They are served with a variety of sweet and sour sauces, ranging from spiced syrups of lime to tamarind and butter. The tomatoes can be prepared a day in advance and baked when needed. They are also delicious served cold with warm flatbread.

for the tomatoes

4 tablespoons olive oil

1 onion, chopped

2 garlic cloves, crushed

1 eggplant, cut into $^1/_2$ inch dice

1 zucchini, cut into $^1/_2$ inch dice

2 green bell peppers, deseeded and cut into $^1/_2$ inch dice

$^1/_2$ pound young leeks, cut into $^1/_2$ inch lengths

1 tablespoon tomato paste

1 tablespoon sugar

$^1/_4$ cup raisins

1 teaspoon orange zest

3 tablespoons chopped fresh cilantro

8 beef tomatoes, tops discarded and
  seeds scooped out

salt and freshly ground black pepper

for the syrup

$^3/_4$ cup white wine vinegar

4 tablespoons corn syrup

good pinch of saffron

$^1/_2$ stick unsalted butter

salt and freshly ground black pepper

for the cashew kibbeh crust

$^1/_2$ cup bulgur, soaked in warm water for 10 minutes

1 cup cashew nuts

$^1/_2$ teaspoon ground cinnamon

$^1/_2$ teaspoon ground cumin

pinch of cayenne pepper

little olive oil

Preheat the oven to 325°F. For the ratatouille, heat half the olive oil in a large pan over a moderate heat, add the onion and garlic, and cook for 2–3 minutes until softened. Add the vegetables, stir well, and cook for 5–6 minutes until they begin to soften. Add the tomato paste, sugar, raisins, and orange zest and stir well. Pour over the remaining oil, cover, reduce the heat, and cook for 20 minutes. Remove and cool slightly before adding the coriander.

Meanwhile, for the basting syrup, boil together the vinegar, corn syrup, and saffron, then whisk in the butter, season, and set aside.

Fill the beef tomatoes with the ratatouille and place in a baking dish. Drizzle the prepared syrup over and around the tomatoes.

For the kibbeh crust, place the cracked wheat, cashew nuts, spices, and olive oil in a food processor and blend together.

Sprinkle the mixture over the tomatoes and bake in the oven for 20 minutes until golden. Allow to cool slightly before serving.

Greek-stuffed onions
with feta cheese custard

A type of modern-day vegetarian moussaka, these sweet oven-roasted
onions are filled with a herby tomato, nut and mushroom filling, then
baked inside a rich feta cheese custard. I like to serve these onions with
some well made pilaf-style rice and a crispy green leaf salad.

8 medium-size red onions, unpeeled

3 tablespoons olive oil

3 tablespoons unsalted butter

1 onion, finely chopped

1 garlic clove, crushed

1 ounce pack of dried porcini mushrooms, soaked in water
    for 30 minutes and drained

$^1/_3$ cup semidry tomatoes in oil, drained and chopped

2 tablespoons chopped fresh flat-leaf parsley

1 tablespoon chopped fresh oregano
    (or $^1/_2$ teaspoon dried)

2 cups fresh white breadcrumbs

$^1/_3$ cup cashew nuts, chopped

pinch of cinnamon

1 free-range egg, lightly beaten

2 ounces feta cheese, grated

salt and freshly ground black pepper

for the feta cheese custard

1 tablespoon unsalted butter

2 tablespoons all-purpose flour

$1^1/_4$ cups milk

$1^1/_4$ cups light cream

1 cup finely grated feta cheese

2 free-range eggs, lightly beaten

salt and freshly ground black pepper

Preheat the oven to 400°F. Remove a good slice off the top of each onion, then
place in a roasting pan or ovenproof dish. Spoon a little water over each onion, then
drizzle over some of the olive oil. Cover the dish with foil and bake for 1 hour or until
the onions are tender. Remove them, leave to cool and peel.

For the stuffing, heat the remaining oil and butter in a large skillet, add the onion
and garlic, and cook until softened and beginning to brown. Add the soaked porcini,
cook for 2–3 minutes, then add the tomatoes and herbs. Finally, add the
breadcrumbs, cashew nuts, and cinnamon. Cook for a further 1 minute and then
transfer to a bowl. Add the beaten egg and cheese, stir until thoroughly combined,
and season to taste.

Carefully remove the centers from each cooked onion. Chop the center and add
to the stuffing mixture. Fill each onion generously with the stuffing, then place in a
suitable-size baking dish, leaving at least $^3/_4$ inch gap between them.

To prepare the custard, place the butter, flour, and milk into a pan. Heat gently,
whisking constantly until the sauce thickens and becomes glossy and smooth.
Reduce the heat, simmer for 1–2 minutes, then remove and cool slightly. Add the
cream and grated feta, beat in the eggs, and season to taste. Pour the cheese
custard carefully between the onions, then return the dish to the oven to bake for
20–25 minutes. Allow to cool slightly before serving.

Fennel and zucchini osso bucco

with castelli gremolata and saffron couscous

For me, fennel is one of the most underrated and underutilized
vegetables there are. Usually partnered with fish, it makes great
vegetarian dishes and this is one of my favorite ways to cook it.

6 tablespoons olive oil

1 onion, finely chopped

1 garlic clove, crushed

$^1/_2$ teaspoon fennel seeds

4 heads of fennel, halved lengthwise, fronds removed

2 zucchini, cut into 2 inch thick slices on bias

1 pound canned tomatoes, chopped

$^1/_2$ cup semidry tomatoes, chopped

1 teaspoon tomato paste

5 tablespoons orange juice

3 cups good vegetable broth

12 black olives, pitted

$^1/_3$ cup raisins

2 tablespoons pine nuts, toasted

2 tablespoons chopped fresh cilantro

for the castelli gremolata

1 cup fresh white breadcrumbs

2 tablespoons freshly grated castelli vegetalia
   (parmesan-style cheese)

$^1/_2$ teaspoon grated lemon zest

$^1/_2$ garlic clove, crushed

$^1/_2$ stick unsalted butter, melted

salt and freshly ground black pepper

for the saffron couscous

1$^1/_4$ cups couscous

1 cup good vegetable broth

1 teaspoon saffron

salt and freshly ground black pepper

Preheat the oven to 400°F. Heat the olive oil in a large skillet, add the onion, garlic,
and fennel seeds, and cook until softened. Add the fennel and cook for 3–4 minutes
until it takes on a little color. Add the zucchini and cook for a further 2–3 minutes.
Add the canned tomatoes, semidry tomatoes, tomato paste, orange juice, and
vegetable broth. Bring to a boil, add the olives, raisins, and pine nuts and cook for
5–6 minutes. Transfer the fennel, zucchini, and sauce to an ovenproof gratin dish.

For the castelli gremolata, combine the breadcrumbs, castelli vegetalia, lemon
zest, garlic, butter, and a little seasoning in a bowl. Sprinkle it evenly over the
vegetables, then place in the oven until the top is crisp and golden.

For the saffron couscous, infuse the vegetable broth with the saffron for
2 minutes and then strain. Place the couscous in a bowl, pour over the hot
vegetable broth, cover with plastic wrap or a lid and leave for 5 minutes. Fork through
the couscous, cover for a futher 2–3 minutes and then season to taste. Place the
couscous on serving plates, top with the fennel and zucchini osso bucco, scatter over
the chopped cilantro, and serve.

Zucchini linguine
with cashew pesto and marinated mushrooms and broccoli

A refreshing variation of the classic pesto. Tossed with raw delicate threads of zucchini, marinated mushrooms, and crunchy broccoli, this is an outstanding plate of color and texture.

for the cashew pesto

1/3 cup raw cashews

2 small garlic cloves, crushed

1 small red chili, deseeded and finely chopped

1 inch piece of fresh ginger, peeled and grated

1/2 cup peanut oil or extra-virgin olive oil

2 tablespoons fresh cilantro leaves

3 tablespoons fresh mint leaves

juice of 1 lime

1/2 pound chestnut mushrooms

1/2 cup extra-virgin olive oil

1 tablespoon shoyu (Japanese soy sauce)

2 garlic cloves, crushed

1 green onion, finely chopped

1 inch piece of fresh ginger, peeled and grated

1/4 pound broccoli, cut into florets

juice of 2 limes

4 crispy and firm courgettes

sea salt and freshly ground black pepper

For the cashew pesto, place the cashews in a blender and blend until broken down. Add the garlic, chili, and ginger and blend to a paste. Add the oil and herbs and blend until puréed. Finish with the lime juice and sea salt. Set aside.

Slice the mushrooms very thinly, place in a bowl, and add the oil, soy sauce, garlic, onion, and ginger. Allow to marinate for 30 minutes or until soft.

Meanwhile, steam the broccoli until it turns bright green but is still crunchy in texture. Quickly remove and add to the mushrooms, along with the lime juice and season to taste. Cut off the ends of the zucchini, then slice, using a kitchen mandolin or knife, as thinly as possible lengthwise into strips or "linguine". Toss with the mushroom and broccoli, adjust the seasoning, and serve.

Grilled paneer cheese
with Indian bread salad

The inspiration for this light main course dish is based on a similar bread salad from Tuscany, called panzanella. I experimented on the idea of adding some Asian flavors on the same theme, and replaced the more usual bread with naan bread. The result was deemed worthy of inclusion, so here it is. These little kebabs taste even better if cooked on a charcoal grill. Indian paneer cheese is similar to Asian tofu in that it has a bland flavor in itself, but often absorbs the flavors of other ingredients well. It is ideal for grilling and roasting, and can be found in Asian food stores.

5 tablespoons fresh mint, finely chopped

4 tablespoons natural yogurt

$^1/_2$ cup finely grated vegetarian mild cheddar cheese

1 inch piece of fresh ginger, peeled and finely grated

2 garlic cloves, crushed

$^1/_2$ teaspoon cumin seeds, toasted

$^1/_2$ teaspoon marjoram, toasted

1$^3/_4$ pounds paneer cheese

little sunflower oil for cooking

salt and freshly ground black pepper

for the bread salad

6 tablespoons sunflower oil

juice of 2 lemons

1 red onion, cut into thin rings

2 red bell peppers, deseeded and chopped

$^3/_4$ pound firm but ripe tomatoes, chopped

2 naan bread, cut or torn into pieces

1 red chili, finely chopped

$^1/_2$ inch piece of fresh ginger, peeled and finely grated

3 tablespoons fresh cilantro, roughly torn

2 tablespoons fresh mint, roughly torn

salt and freshly ground black pepper

large wooden bamboo skewers, soaked (see PG TIPS)

Mix together the mint, yogurt, grated cheddar, and ginger in a bowl. Add the garlic, cumin, marjoram, and a little seasoning to form a thick paste (adding a little more cheddar if necessary).

Cut the paneer into 3 inch x 2 inch blocks, and then with a sharp small knife, cut down each cheese into three sections, without cutting right through the base, about $^1/_3$ inch from the bottom. Using a small palette knife, thickly smear the insides of all the cheeses with the paste, then skewer two blocks lengthwise with a soaked skewer (or two) to secure them tightly while cooking.

For the bread salad, combine the oil, lemon juice, and 2 tablespoons of water in a large bowl. Add the vegetables and toss well. Add the naan bread, chili, ginger, and herbs and mix well. Allow to stand for about 15 minutes for the flavors to meld and season to taste. Heat a ridged skillet with a little oil. When hot, place the paneer skewers on it and cook for 3–4 minutes, turning them regularly, until lightly charred all over.

Share the salad among four serving plates or bowls. Remove the cheese from the skillet, arrange on the salad and serve immediately.

PG TIPS Wooden skewers, when placed on a charcoal grill, have the tendency to burn and fall apart. To counteract this, simply soak the skewers in water for 24 hours and use on the grill without any worries.

Plantain empanadas
with mango and corn salsa and arroz verde

It is vitally important that the plantains are just ripe (yellow with black mottling), as overripe black plantains are too starchy to wrap the beans.

3 yellow-black mottled plantains (about 2 pounds)

1 1/2 cups black beans

vegetable oil for cooking

1 onion, chopped

2 garlic cloves, crushed

1 green chili, deseeded and finely chopped

1 green bell pepper, deseeded and finely chopped

1 teaspoon ground cumin

2 tablespoons honey

1 tablespoon white wine vinegar

1/4 pound feta cheese, crumbled

1 cup all-purpose flour

fresh cilantro leaves to garnish

1/2 cup sour cream (optional)

salt and freshly ground black pepper

for the arroz verde (green rice)

1 small onion, finely chopped

1 green chili, deseeded and quartered

3 garlic cloves, crushed

6 tablespoons fresh cilantro leaves

2 cups good vegetable broth

2 tablespoons vegetable oil

1 cup long-grain white rice

for the mango and corn salsa

8 ounces canned corn, drained

1 mango, pitted and cut into 1/3 inch dice

2 tablespoons chopped fresh cilantro

2 firm but ripe tomatoes, cut into 1/3 inch dice

1 shallot, chopped

1 garlic clove, crushed

juice of 2 limes

2 tablespoons maple syrup

Preheat the oven to 425°F. Using a small knife, cut a slit through the peel of each plantain from top to bottom along the inner curve, then place in a baking pan. Bake in the oven for up to 50 minutes. Leave to cool for 1 hour.

Cook the black beans in boiling salted water for 30–40 minutes and drain.

Heat a little vegetable oil in a skillet, add the onion, garlic, chili, green bell pepper, and cumin and cook over a low heat until tender. Add the beans and cook for 5 minutes for the flavors to infuse, then add the honey and vinegar. Cook for a further 1 minute, transfer to a bowl, and leave to cool. Mash the mixture finely with a potato masher and season to taste. Add the feta and set aside.

Peel the plantains, then blend in a food processor until they come together like dough. Remove, add the flour, and roll the dough in lightly oiled hands into eight equal-size balls. Roll out the dough balls with a rolling pin to about 1/2 inch thick. Fill each of the rolled dough balls with a good spoonful of the black bean mixture and fold over carefully to form pastries, crimping the edges with your thumb and finger to seal. Prepare all the same way. Refrigerate until required.

For the green rice, place the onion, chili, garlic, cilantro, and half of the broth in a food processor, blend well until smooth, and season with a little salt and pepper. Heat the oil in a heavy-based pan and add the rice, stirring constantly for 1 minute. Add the green broth and the remaining vegetable broth, bring to a boil, and simmer for 20 minutes. Remove the pan from the heat but keep covered, allowing the rice to steam for a further 5 minutes.

For the salsa, mix all the ingredients together in a bowl and season to taste.

Heat 2–3 inches of vegetable oil in a deep-fat fryer or large pan to about 325°F, add the empanadas and fry for about 2–3 minutes until golden. Transfer to paper towels to drain. Serve the empanadas on a bed of the green rice, with the cool tasting salsa alongside and garnish with the cilantro leaves and a good dollop of the sour cream, if desired.

Pastry

Who can resist a dish of any sort made with pastry? I know I can't! There is something so comforting about food encased in a light crisp, or rich buttery crust. The fillings can be as varied as your imagination and taste. Using pastry in vegetarian cooking is particularly successful—it not only gives focus to a dish, but also adds substance and the necessary protein needed for a balanced vegetarian diet.

Grated celeriac, camembert, and prune tarts
with warm lentil vinaigrette

This lovely celeriac tart makes enough for four main courses or six as an
appetizer. I discovered the flavorsome marriage of camembert cheeses
and prunes at a promotion launch I prepared at the hotel last year.

10 ounces prepared fresh shortcrust pastry

1/2 stick unsalted butter

1 small celeriac, peeled and coarsely grated

6 ounces crème fraîche (or heavy cream)

1/2 pound firm but ripe camembert, cut into 1/2 inch dice

1/4 pound ready-to-eat prunes (pits removed), chopped

3 free-range eggs

1 free-range egg yolk

salt, freshly ground black pepper, and ground nutmeg

for the lentil vinaigrette

1 1/4 cups puy lentils

2 garlic cloves, crushed

2 teaspoons Dijon mustard

2 tablespoons balsamic vinegar

6 tablespoons extra-virgin olive oil

1 small red onion, sliced

1/4 pound baby spinach leaves

3 tablespoons watercress, tough stalks removed

salt and freshly cracked black pepper

10 inch pie pan with removable base

serves 4–6

Preheat the oven to 400°F. Roll out the pastry to 1/3 inch thick and use it to line a
greased loose-bottomed tart tin. Prick with a fork all over and then chill for 20
minutes. Line the pastry bottom with baking parchment and fill with baking beans.
Bake blind for 20 minutes. Carefully remove the beans and parchment, then return
the pan to the oven to cook for a further 5 minutes. Remove and cool slightly.

Melt the butter in a pan, add the celeriac, and cook over a gentle heat for
5 minutes. Pour in the crème fraîche and simmer for 10 minutes. Remove from the
heat, add half the camembert, the prunes, stir in the eggs, and mix well. Season with
salt, pepper, and nutmeg. Pour the mixture into the pastry case, dot with the
remaining camembert, and cook for 20 minutes or until firm to the touch. Remove
from the oven and leave to cool.

Meanwhile, place the lentils in a pan, cover with water, bring to a boil and simmer
for 20 minutes. Top up with more water if necessary.

In a bowl, whisk together the garlic, mustard, vinegar, and olive oil. When the
lentils are cooked, drain them thoroughly, then add the dressing, and mix well. Add
the remaining ingredients, toss together gently, and season with salt and freshly
cracked black pepper. Serve the tart, cut into wedges, with the warm lentil vinaigrette.

Chèvre and polenta tart

with caramelized onions and grilled vegetables

The chèvre and polenta filling is lovely served on its own, without the crisp pastry tarts. This dish is enjoyed by many vegetarian diners at The Lanesborough, where it has been a favorite for many years.

12 ounces prepared shortcrust pastry

2 1/2 cups milk or water

1 1/3 cups canned corn, well drained

3/4 cup quick-cook polenta

2 tablespoons unsalted butter

1/4 pound herb chèvre

4 tablespoons olive oil

2 red onions, thinly sliced

2 teaspoons superfine sugar

2 tablespoons balsamic vinegar

4 baby zucchini, halved horizontally

2 portobello mushrooms, thickly sliced

4 plum tomatoes, halved

2 red bell peppers, halved, deseeded and cut
  into thick strips

2 garlic cloves, crushed

4 tablespoons basil pesto (bought or homemade—see
  PG TIPS page 103)

12 fresh basil leaves

salt and freshly ground black pepper

4 x 1 1/2 inch x 3 inch diameter tartlet pans or pastry rings

Preheat the oven to 375ºF. Roll out the pastry to 1/4 inch thick to line the tartlet pans or pastry rings. Fill with a little baking parchment and baking beans and bake blind for 10–12 minutes. Remove the baking beans and parchment and return to the oven for a further 5 minutes. Remove and cool before removing the pastry shells from the pans. These tartlets can be prepared in advance.

Bring the milk or water to a boil, add the corn and cook for 5 minutes. Transfer to a food processor and blend to a smooth liquid. Return the corn milk to the pan, bring to a boil, and stir in the polenta to a smooth paste. Reduce the heat and cook for 10–12 minutes, stirring frequently. Add the butter and chèvre and season to taste. Keep hot.

Heat the olive oil in a pan, add the onions, and cook over a moderate heat for 5 minutes until softened. Add the sugar and vinegar and cook for a further 10–12 minutes, stirring occasionally until soft and caramelized. Set aside.

Place the vegetables in a bowl, add the garlic and remaining olive oil and toss together. Heat a ridged skillet and, when hot, add the vegetables and fry, turning them regularly, until cooked and lightly caramelized.

Fill the cooked tartlets with some caramelized onions then top with the chèvre polenta, leveling off the surface with a wet palette knife. Top each tartlet with a heaped pile of grilled vegetables, drizzle the basil pesto over and around the tartlets. Garnish with fresh basil leaves and serve.

PG TIPS For a tasty variation to this dish, why not top the vegetables with a slice or two of thin Tuscan scamorza—a soft, delicate cheese popular throughout Italy.

Torta di scalogni

A simple torta or Italian-style freeform pie made from candied shallots with raisins and delectable Italian taleggio cheese wrapped in a thin pastry, then baked until crispy. Ideally served hot from the oven, it's also good cold served with a crisp salad as part of an interesting picnic. If you don't have a pizza pan, use a flat cookie sheet and cut the dough to the right size.

for the dough

2 cups all-purpose flour, plus little extra for dusting

1/2 teaspoon salt

3 tablespoons extra-virgin olive oil

for the filling

2 tablespoons unsalted butter

1 pound small shallots, peeled

1/4 cup raisins

1 tablespoon caster sugar

1 tablespoon red wine vinegar

3/4 cup roasted vegetable broth (see page 189)

6 ounces taleggio cheese, cut into small dice

2 tablespoons walnuts, roughly chopped

1 tablespoon marjoram

13 inch round pizza sheet

serves 6

Mix together the flour and salt in a large bowl and make a well in the center. Add the oil and 1/2 cup cold water a little at a time and bring in the sides. Carefully work the dough until it just holds together. Knead the dough until smooth and elastic, then shape into a ball and return to the bowl. Cover and refrigerate for up to 2 hours.

For the filling, heat the butter in a large nonstick pan and, when hot, add the shallots and raisins and roll them in the butter for 1 minute. Sprinkle over the sugar and lightly caramelize for 2–3 minutes. Add the vinegar and vegetable broth and bring to a boil. Cover and cook over a moderate heat for 15 minutes until the shallots are soft and the liquid all but evaporated. Tip into a bowl and leave to cool.

Preheat the oven to 350°F. Lightly oil and flour a large 13 inch round pizza pan. Split the dough in two and roll one piece to cover the pizza pan. Cut off any overhanging dough with a knife.

Add the taleggio, walnuts, and marjoram to the filling and mix lightly together. Top the rolled dough with the filling, leaving a 1 inch border of crust exposed around the edge. Roll out the second half of the dough, trim to a 12 inch circle and place on top of the filling. Wet the edge of the bottom crust, then fold in over the top and crimp to seal. Use a fork to pierce several holes all over the torta to allow the steam to escape. Gently brush the torta all over with a little olive oil. Bake in the oven for about 30 minutes until crispy and golden, then remove, and leave to cool slightly. Cut into wedges with a sharp knife and serve.

PG TIPS   You can make the tortas individually and vary the fillings—some of my favorites are mozzarella and artichoke or spinach and potato, but the variations are only limited by your imagination.

Mediterranean pisto pie
with tapenade and salmorejo sauce

A pisto is a typical Spanish-style ratatouille made with wonderfully
colorful vegetables and bursting with flavor. Good on its own, I think
when wrapped in flaky buttery pastry it is unbeatable. A classic salmorejo
sauce completes this dish fit for any table. Tapenade is a spicy olive paste
flavored with capers and is available from supermarkets.

4 tablespoons olive oil

1 eggplant, cut into large dice

1 red onion, thinly sliced

4 garlic cloves, thinly sliced

2 zucchini, sliced

1 red bell pepper, deseeded and finely sliced

1 red chili, deseeded and finely chopped

1 teaspoon picked fresh oregano

1 pound prepared puff pastry

3 tablespoons tapenade

little beaten egg

1 teaspoon sesame seeds

salt and freshly ground black pepper

for the salmorejo sauce

4 ripe tomatoes

1 onion, finely chopped

1 red chili, deseeded and finely chopped

1 garlic clove, crushed

2 tablespoons olive oil

1 tablespoon white wine vinegar

1 tablespoon chopped fresh flat-leaf parsley

Heat the olive oil in a large skillet and, when hot, add the eggplant and fry for
2–3 minutes. Add the remaining vegetables and fry over a moderate heat until all
the vegetables are softened. Season to taste, add the oregano, and mix well together.
Leave to cool.

Preheat the oven to 400°F. On a lightly floured surface, roll out half the pastry to
a rectangle measuring about 8 inches long and 6 inches wide and transfer to a large
cookie sheet. Spread the tapenade over the pastry base, then spoon over the
vegetables, leaving a 1 inch border around the edge. Roll out the remaining pastry to
the same size and use to cover the first. Brush the edges with water or beaten egg,
then press together to seal. Lightly mark squares on the pastry with the back of a
knife, brush with beaten egg, and sprinkle with sesame seeds. Place in the oven to
bake for 30–35 minutes or until risen and golden brown.

Meanwhile, for the salmorejo sauce, cut the tomatoes in half and place them on
a cookie sheet. Bake for 15–20 minutes until charred on both sides (or place under
a preheated hot broiler), remove, and leave to cool. When the tomatoes are cold,
peel and deseed them and place in a small food processor with the remaining
ingredients, except the parsley. Blend to a smooth sauce, season to taste, transfer
to a bowl, and add the parsley. Cut the pie into sections and serve with the
salmorejo sauce.

PG TIPS   Some new potatoes and buttered fresh spinach with toasted pine nuts
make a great accompaniment.

Potato and leek flamiche
with celeriac and carrot remoulade

Flamiche can be either a sweet or savory tart from northern France. The
best known variety is made with leeks, sometimes with the addition of a
local strong cheese called maroilles (a particular favorite of mine).
Flamiche is the Flemish word for cake.

10 ounces prepared puff pastry

2 tablespoons unsalted butter

1/2 pound new potatoes, peeled and thinly sliced
   to 1/2 inch thick

1 pound small leeks, sliced

1/2 cup crème fraîche (or heavy cream)

2 teaspoons Dijon mustard

1 tablespoon chopped fresh tarragon

1 free-range egg yolk mixed with 1 tablespoon water

salt, freshly ground black pepper, and ground nutmeg

for the remoulade

1/2 small celeriac, peeled

1 Granny Smith apple, cored and peeled

1 carrot, peeled

1/2 cup good quality mayonnaise

1 teaspoon Dijon mustard

1 teaspoon lemon juice

2 teaspoons small fresh tarragon leaves

salt and freshly ground black pepper

serves 6

Preheat the oven to 425°F. Divide the pastry into two then roll it out about 1/5 inch thick and cut out 2 x 10 inch circles (using a 10 inch plate as a guide). Prick both circles with a fork and chill in the fridge while you make the filling.

   Melt the butter in a large saucepan, add the potato slices, leeks, and 2 tablespoons of water, cover, and boil rapidly for 1 minute. Remove the lid, add the crème fraîche and mustard, and cook for a further 5–6 minutes until the vegetables are tender and the cream all but gone. Remove from the heat and leave to cool. Add the tarragon and season well with salt, freshly ground pepper, and ground nutmeg.

   When cold, place the vegetable mixture in a dome shape on one of the pastry circles, leaving a 1 inch border around the edge. Brush the edges with water. Top with the other pastry circle, lightly press together and, with a sharp small knife, make vertical cuts along the pastry edges. Transfer to a greased cookie sheet. With a small sharp knife, score the top of the pie from the center outward, to create a spoke effect. Brush all over with the beaten egg and cook in the oven for 25–30 minutes until golden and flaky.

   Meanwhile, for the remoulade, cut the celeriac, apple and carrot into fine strips or julienne on a kitchen mandolin. Place in a bowl, add the mayonnaise, salt, pepper, and mustard and cream together gently—the vegetables and apple should bound in the mayonnaise. Finally add the lemon juice and mix again.

   Cut the flamiche into wedges, garnish with the remoulade alongside, and scatter the tarragon leaves over the top. Serve immediately.

PG TIPS   When using herbs in salads I rarely chop them, preferring to use small ones, leaving them whole to get the fullest flavor from them.

Parsnip tatin

with pickled beets and onion confit

Delicious little individual savory tatins of parsnip caramelized in a sweet and sour spicy mixture, topped with pickled beets. Good parsnips are available all year round now, but I still find the best follow a winter cold snap to bring out their best flavor.

4 medium-size parsnips, halved lengthwise with
  center cores removed

2 tablespoons olive oil

3 tablespoons soft brown sugar

4 tablespoons white wine vinegar

juice of 1 lemon

1 teaspoon ground cumin

1 teaspoon candied stem ginger, finely chopped

1 pound prepared puff pastry

2 pickled beets, drained and finely shredded

few mixed salad leaves

salt and freshly ground black pepper

for the onion confit

4 tablespoons olive oil

1/2 pound red onions, halved and sliced

1 teaspoon soft brown sugar

2 garlic cloves, crushed

pinch of red chili flakes

1 teaspoon lemon thyme leaves (optional)

4 x 4 inch square pans

Preheat the oven to 400°F. Toss the parsnips with the olive oil in a roasting pan, season lightly, and place in the oven to cook for 30 minutes, turning them occasionally.

For the onion confit, heat the oil in a skillet, add the onions, and cook over a moderate heat for 5–6 minutes or until starting to soften. Add the sugar, garlic, and chili flakes, lower the heat and add 4 tablespoons of water. Cook for 15 minutes until they become lightly caramelized and tender. Add the lemon thyme if desired. Remove the onions with a slotted spoon and leave to cool.

Heat the pan again over a high heat, add the sugar, vinegar, lemon juice, cumin, and ginger, and simmer for 6–8 minutes until caramelized. Add the roasted parsnip and roll in the glaze syrup for 1 minute. Remove and set aside.

Roll out the pastry to about 1/5 inch thick, then using a 5 inch cutter, cut out four circles. Arrange the caramelized parsnips (cutside up) in the bottom of the pans and spoon over any juices from the roasting pan. Top with the onion confit, pressing down lightly, then lay the cut pastry circles on top, press down, and bake for 20 minutes or until golden and puffed. When cooked, leave to cool slightly before inverting them onto four serving plates. Drizzle over any remaining cooking juices and top with the pickled beets and salad leaves. Serve immediately.

Cauliflower singaras

with subj chaat and cilantro chutney

Singaras, like their cousins samosas, are an everyday snack sold by street
vendors in India. Enjoy them here with delicious accompaniments.

for the singaras

1 cauliflower, cut into florets

2 tablespoons ghee or sunflower oil

1 small onion, finely chopped

1 garlic clove, crushed

1/2 inch piece of fresh ginger, peeled and finely grated

1 small hot green chili, finely chopped

1/2 teaspoon ground cumin

1/2 teaspoon ground coriander

1/2 teaspoon garam masala

3 tablespoons chopped fresh cilantro

2 tablespoons chopped fresh mint

lemon juice

1 package of samosa pastry

vegetable oil for deep-frying

salt and freshly ground black pepper

for the subj chaat

5 tablespoons tamarind pulp

5 tablespoons brown sugar, or to taste

*2 red bell peppers, roasted, deseeded,
    and cut into 1/2 inch dice*

*1 yellow bell pepper, roasted, deseeded,
    and cut into 1/2 inch dice*

1/4 pound pineapple, cut into 1/2 inch dice

1 red onion, sliced

pinch of ground cumin

pinch of chaat masala

salt

for the cilantro chutney

3 tablespoons cilantro, chopped

2 small green chilies, deseeded and chopped

3 tablespoons lemon juice

1/2 onion, chopped

2 tablespoons peanuts

Cook the cauliflower in boiling water for 6–8 minutes and remove with a slotted
spoon into cold water. Drain and dry.

Heat the oil in a large skillet, add the onion and garlic and fry over a moderate
heat until lightly golden. Add the ginger and chili and cook for 2–3 minutes. Add the
cauliflower, cumin, coriander, garam masala, and 1/2 cup water and cook over a high
heat until all the liquid has gone and the cauliflower is slightly mushy. Finally add the
herbs, lemon juice, and season to taste. Transfer to a bowl and leave to cool.

Using one strip of the pastry at a time, place 1 tablespoon of the filling mixture at
one end. Diagonally fold up the pastry to form an enclosed triangle. Moisten the end
of the strip with water and press lightly to secure. Prepare all the singaras in the
same manner.

For the subj chaat, place the tamarind and 1 1/2 cups water in a pan, bring to a
boil and simmer for 10–12 minutes until the tamarind coats the base of a spoon.
Add the sugar, or more to taste, and a little salt and leave to cool. Place the bell
peppers, pineapple, and onion in a bowl and add enough of the tamarind sauce to
coat the mixture. Season with a little cumin and chaat masala.

Heat the oil in a small deep-fryer or large pan to 325°F and fry the singaras in
small batches until golden and crispy. Remove with a slotted spoon and drain on
paper towels.

For the chutney, place all the ingredients together in a blender and blend to a
chunky consistency. The chutney will keep well in a storage jar in the fridge for
4–5 days.

Place a pile of the subj chaat on a plate, place the singaras on top and drizzle
over a little of the chutney. Alternatively, serve separately.

Potato pizza bianco
with mozzarella, beet, and rosemary

A tasty pizza-style flatbread made of mashed potato, topped with sweet beet and mozzarella cheese. It makes a great light lunch option or unusual vegetarian starter. Always use the best quality buffalo mozzarella you can find because there are many cheap inferior makes on the market—it will make such a difference.

for the flatbread
$^1/_2$ stick unsalted butter
$^1/_2$ cup self-rising flour
pinch of salt
1 cup hot, freshly cooked mashed potato
1 free-range egg, beaten

for the topping
2 buffalo mozzarella, thinly sliced
2 medium-size beets, roasted (see page 77)
  and peeled
2 tablespoons olive oil
1 teaspoon fresh rosemary, roughly chopped
$^1/_2$ cup crème fraîche

Preheat the oven to 425°F. In a bowl, rub the butter with the flour, add a pinch of salt and the hot mashed potato and lightly bind together. Turn the mixture out onto a lightly floured surface and knead it lightly. Using a floured rolling pin, roll out the dough into a large circle approximately $^1/_2$ inch thick. Using a floured cookie cutter, cut out 4 x 5 inch circles, then brush them liberally all over with beaten egg.

Place the potato flatbreads on a large well greased cookie sheet and lay the mozzarella slices evenly over each flatbread. Slice the beets thinly and place on top. Sprinkle over the olive oil and rosemary and place in the oven to bake for 15–18 minutes or until the potato bases are golden and crispy. To serve, top with a good dollop of crème fraîche.

Quail's eggs béarnaise tartlets

with mushroom and olive duxelles, and asparagus au beurre

A delicious rich, buttery herb sauce coating soft-boiled quail's eggs in a crisp
pastry tart shell. An impressive appetizer for a special occasion dinner party.

10 ounces prepared shortcrust pastry

12 quail's eggs

12 cooked asparagus tips, halved lengthwise

1 tablespoon unsalted butter

salt and freshly ground black pepper

for the mushroom and olive duxelles

1 tablespoon unsalted butter

1 shallot, finely chopped

1 teaspoon fresh thyme leaves

6 ounces flat mushrooms, finely chopped

1 ounce pitted black olives, finely chopped

1 teaspoon honey

1/2 cup dry white wine

1/2 cup fresh white breadcrumbs

salt and freshly ground black pepper

for the béarnaise sauce

2 tablespoons white wine vinegar

2 tablespoons water

1/2 teaspoon crushed white peppercorns

3 free-range egg yolks

6 ounces unsalted butter, clarified (see PG TIPS)

2 tablespoons chopped fresh tarragon

1 tablespoon chopped fresh flat-leaf parsley

salt and freshly ground black pepper

4 x 3 1/2 inch tartlet pans

Preheat the oven to 375°F. Roll out the pastry to line the tartlet pans. Fill with baking parchment and baking beans and bake blind for 10 minutes. Remove the beans and parchment and return to the oven for a further 5 minutes. Leave to cool.

For the mushroom and olive duxelles, heat the butter in a skillet, add the shallots and thyme, and cook for 1 minute. Add the mushrooms, olives, and honey and cook for 4–5 minutes until golden brown. Add the wine and cook for a further 1 minute. Finally add the breadcrumbs, mix well, season to taste, and keep warm.

For the béarnaise sauce, place the vinegar, water, and peppercorns in a small pan and boil vigorously until it has reduced to 1 tablespoon. Remove from the heat and leave to cool, then strain into a heatproof bowl. Add the egg yolks to the liquid and whisk together. Set the bowl over a pan of simmering water, with the base just above the water. Whisk the egg mixture for 5–6 minutes or until it becomes thick and ribbon-like, creamy, and smooth in texture. Remove from the heat and slowly add the butter in a thin stream, whisking until the sauce is thick and glossy. Add the herbs and season to taste. Keep warm over a bain marie.

Boil the quail's eggs for 2 minutes in boiling water, then immediately remove them with a slotted spoon and plunge in cold water to refresh them. While they are still warm, carefully peel them.

To finish the dish, fill each tartlet shell with some olive and mushroom duxelles and top each with three quail's eggs. Coat the eggs completely with béarnaise sauce, then place under a hot broiler to glaze for about 30 seconds until beautifully golden. Heat the asparagus tips in hot butter and season to taste. Place a line of asparagus tips on each plate, top with an egg-filled tartlet and serve. Delicious!

PG TIPS   If you want to prepare your quail's eggs in advance, a little tip is to cook them as usual, then immerse them immediately into a mixture of cold water and some distilled vinegar and leave for 10 minutes before peeling. To serve, simply reheat for 15 seconds in boiling water.

To clarify butter, heat the butter in a pan until bubbling and skim off any impurities that rise to the surface with a ladle or large spoon. Slowly pour off the liquid butter, leaving the milky white sediment in the pan. It is now ready for use.

Kadaifi apple fritters
with pickled blue cheese salad

Kadaifi (or kataifi) is a type of phyllo pastry that is finely shredded and makes an interesting wrapping for many dishes. It is available from Middle Eastern or Greek stores.

for the kadaifi fritters

1 Granny Smith apple, cored and finely diced

juice of $^1/_2$ lemon

$^1/_4$ pound creamy blue cheese, crumbled

$^1/_2$ teaspoon Dijon mustard

pinch of paprika

3 cups fresh white breadcrumbs

1 free-range egg yolk

little flour

4 ounces kadaifi pastry

3 tablespoons unsalted butter, melted

vegetable oil for deep-frying

salt, freshly ground black pepper, and ground nutmeg

for the pickled blue cheese salad

2 tablespoons superfine sugar

4 tablespoons red wine vinegar

1 carrot, peeled

3 ounces celeriac, peeled

1 red onion, peeled and thinly sliced

3 ounces baby spinach leaves

2 tablespoons fresh flat-leaf parsley leaves

3 tablespoons arugula leaves

3 ounces blue cheese, frozen for 10 minutes and shaved

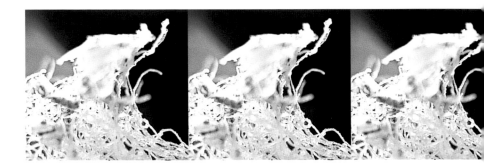

Coat the apple with the lemon juice and toss together for 1 minute.

For the kadaifi, place the crumbled cheese in a bowl and add the diced apple, the mustard, paprika, and breadcrumbs and finally the egg yolk. Season and bring the mixture together to a thick paste that holds its shape. Refrigerate for 2 hours, then remove, and shape into eight small patties. Dust with a little flour.

Carefully unwrap the pastry and spread it out onto a work surface. Liberally brush the pastry strands with melted butter, then wrap the patties in it making sure the pastry completely covers them. Set aside.

For the salad, heat the sugar and vinegar in a pan and boil for 1 minute. Using a kitchen mandolin or sharp knife, shred the carrot and celeriac in a bowl and add the thinly sliced onion. Pour over the hot vinegar and leave to cool. When cold, add the spinach, parsley, and arugula and toss well together. Finally add half the cheese.

To serve, deep- or shallow-fry the kadaifi fritters for about 3–4 minutes until golden and crispy, remove, and drain on kitchen paper. Divide the salad and pile high on four plates, place two fritters per person on top of each salad and sprinkle over the remaining shaved cheese. Alternatively serve the salad separately.

Open-faced spinach and feta sambusak
with preserved lemon salsa

Preserving lemons in salt is commonplace in Middle Eastern countries and it adds spicy overtones to the lemon's sourness. They are easy to prepare at home but take a while to mature (up to three months). However, there are some good quality ones on the market.

for the sambusak

2 tablespoons olive oil

3 tablespoons pine nuts

1 large onion, thinly sliced

1 teaspoon allspice

1/2 teaspoon cumin seeds

1/2 pound spinach, washed

1/3 cup semidry tomatoes, chopped

1/2 teaspoon lemon zest

10 ounces prepared puff pastry

6 ounces Greek feta cheese, crumbled

little beaten egg

salt and freshly ground black pepper

for the preserved lemon salsa

3 tablespoons extra-virgin olive oil

juice of 2 lemons

1 garlic clove, crushed

*1 small red bell pepper, halved, deseeded, and
    cut into 1/3 inch dice*

1 red onion, finely chopped

1/2 cucumber, deseeded and cut into 1/3 inch dice

1 teaspoon preserved lemon, cut into 1/5 inch dice

3 tablespoons chopped fresh cilantro

2 plum tomatoes, cut into 1/3 inch dice

pinch of sugar

salt and freshly ground black pepper

Preheat the oven to 375°F. Heat the olive oil in a skillet and, when hot, add the pine nuts and cook until golden all over. Remove and drain, reserving the oil. Return the oil to the pan on the heat, add the onion and cook over a moderate heat for about 8–10 minutes until golden all over. Add the allspice and cumin seeds, cook for a further 1 minute, remove with a slotted spoon, and set aside.

Once again return the pan to the heat, add the spinach and cook for 3–4 minutes until wilted and all the excess moisture absorbed. Return the onions and nuts to the pan and add the semidry tomatoes. Cook together for a further 2 minutes. Add the lemon zest, season to taste, and set aside to cool.

Roll out the pastry 1/5 inch thick, then cut out 4 x 31/2 inch circles. Lay out the circles on a flat surface, then divide the spinach mixture equally between them. Divide the feta into four equal amounts and place on top of the spinach. Brush the edges of the pastry with the beaten egg and bring them up to the center, pressing them lightly, leaving the center of the pastry open. Place the sambusaks on a nonstick cookie sheet and bake in the oven for 15–20 minutes until golden and flaky.

Meanwhile, for the salsa, mix the olive oil, lemon juice, and garlic in a bowl. Add the remaining ingredients, toss well together, and season to taste. To serve, place the sambusaks onto four serving plates and dress with the salsa dressing. It is important to eat the sambusaks warm while the cheese remains soft and creamy.

Portobello tart gratin
in hazelnut pastry with parsley and garlic sauce

Any combination of mushroom, garlic, and parsley is always a winner. If fontina cheese is unavailable, use an alternative easy melting cheese such as emmental or gruyère.

for the portobello tart

1 1/4 cups all-purpose flour

3/4 cup ground hazelnuts

6 ounces unsalted butter, chilled and cut into small dice

1 small free-range egg, lightly beaten

1 garlic clove

2 tablespoons olive oil

8 medium-size portobello mushrooms, with stems

1 shallot, finely chopped

1 teaspoon fresh thyme leaves

2 ounces fontina cheese, thinly sliced

1 tablespoon fresh flat-leaf parsley leaves, chopped

salt and freshly ground black pepper

for the parsley and garlic sauce

2 tablespoons fresh flat-leaf parsley leaves

1 garlic clove, crushed

1/2 cup light cream

1/2 cup vegetable broth

2 tablespoons unsalted butter, chilled and cut
  into small pieces

salt and freshly ground black pepper

For the pastry, place the flour, salt, and hazelnuts in a bowl, add the chilled diced butter, and work with your fingertips until it resembles breadcrumbs. Add the egg and work it into a dough, kneading gently. Refrigerate for 30 minutes.

Preheat the oven to 400°F. Clean the mushrooms with a wet cloth and cut in half vertically through the stems to yield sixteen halves. Crush the garlic clove with the blade of a knife. Rub the inside of a large nonstick pan all over with the garlic clove, then discard it. Heat the oil in the pan and, when hot, add the mushrooms, shallot, and thyme and fry over a high heat until golden all over. Season to taste and keep warm.

Roll out the pastry 1/5 inch thick, then cut into 4 x 4 inch long x 2 inch wide strips. Place on a cookie sheet and bake in the oven for 10–12 minutes. Remove and top each cooked strip with some fontina cheese slices, then top each with the mushrooms. Return to the oven for 2 minutes.

For the sauce, place the parsley and garlic in a small food processor and blend to a purée. Add the cream and broth, then blend again until very smooth. Heat in a pan with the butter until boiling and season to taste. Place the tarts onto four serving plates and spoon around the parsley and garlic sauce. Sprinkle the chopped parsley over the mushrooms and serve immediately.

Desserts

There is nothing more pleasing, I am told by
enthusiastic home cooks, than creating 5-star
desserts in the home. Desserts may be the
parting memory of any great dinner party, but
from my experience, they are the most desired
and anticipated offering of all the courses.
I have given you some unusual, yet accessible,
dishes here to give that wow factor to the end
of a meal.

Lavender yogurt cheesecake
with kaffir lime-flavored strawberries

A simple and delightful summer dessert. Everyone loves cheesecake in
one form or another—here lavender adds a touch of summer elegance.

for the kaffir lime-flavored strawberries

1/2 cup superfine sugar

zest and juice of 2 limes

6 kaffir lime leaves, torn

1 cup fresh strawberries, hulled

1/2 stick unsalted butter

1/2 teaspoon dried lavender flowers, finely crushed
* (plus some lavender sprigs for decorating)*

1 cup graham crackers, finely crushed

1/3 cup superfine sugar

1/2 pound good quality cream cheese

1 cup thick set natural yogurt

3/4 cup heavy cream

8 inch flan ring

For the strawberries, bring the sugar and 1 cup water to a boil, making sure the sugar has completely melted and formed a light syrup. Add the lime zest and juice and kaffir lime leaves and leave to cool. Halve the strawberries, place in a bowl, and pour over the lime syrup. Refrigerate overnight.

For the cheesecake, melt the butter in a pan, add the lavender flowers and remove from the heat. Stir in the crushed graham crackers and 2 tablespoons of sugar and mix well together. While still warm, press the biscuits into the base of a flan ring. Refrigerate for 2 hours to set.

In a bowl, beat the cream cheese, the remaining sugar, and yogurt until smooth.

In another bowl, whip the heavy cream until half whipped and just holding its shape, then gently fold into the yogurt mixture until amalgamated. Spread the mixture over the lavender crumb base and smooth over the surface with a palette knife. Return to the fridge for 1 hour or until easy to serve. Decorate the cheesecake with marinated strawberries and fresh lavender.

Soft cheese panna cotta
with pineapple and raspberries

Brillat-Savarin is a delicious soft French triple-cream cheese. It is creamy in texture, which makes it ideal for panna cotta. For me, Del Monte pineapples are the juiciest and sweetest, but they are expensive.

1 1/4 cups heavy cream

1 vanilla bean, split with seeds removed and reserved

1 piece of lemon peel

1/2 cup superfine sugar

1 teaspoon vege-gel (vegetarian alternative to gelatin)

1 1/3 cups soft Brillat-Savarin cheese

1/2 fresh pineapple, skin removed

3/4 cup sugar

3 tablespoons Malibu liqueur

1/2 pound fresh raspberries

1 teaspoon chopped pistachios (optional)

6 x 3 1/2 ounce molds or cups

serves 6

Place the cream in a pan with the vanilla bean, seeds, lemon peel, and sugar. Heat until boiling, then remove and leave to infuse for 20 minutes. Remove the vanilla bean and lemon peel from the cream and sprinkle over the vege-gel. Slowly reheat the cream, whisking well and constantly until the mixture thickens. Remove from the heat, whisk in the cheese, then quickly pour into six oiled molds or cups. Leave to cool, then refrigerate overnight to set.

For the fruits, cut the pineapple into small pieces. Bring 2/3 cup water and the sugar to the boil, remove from the heat, and leave to go cold. Add the Malibu liqueur, pineapple, and raspberries and chill for 1 hour.

To serve, loosen the panna cotta from the molds and place on individual serving plates. Decorate with the fruit and pistachios.

Banana tofu fool

with green tea sherbet and chocolate sauce

An interesting dessert for tofu lovers. Green tea is served in Japanese homes as a sign of welcome and is becoming increasingly popular. It is wonderful when infused into a sherbet, as used in this dessert.

for the green tea sherbet

1/4 cup caster superfine sugar

2 tablespoons glucose

2 teaspoons green tea leaves (or powder)

for the banana tofu fool

1/4 pound silken tofu

1/2 cup soy milk

1/2 teaspoon vanilla extract

1 cup Greek natural yogurt

2 bananas, peeled and chopped

zest and juice of 1 lemon

fresh mint leaves

for the chocolate sauce

2 ounces good quality bittersweet chocolate
  (70% cocoa solids)

1/2 cup heavy cream

1/2 teaspoon vanilla extract

4 martini glasses or serving dishes

For the green tea sherbet, place 2 cups water, the sugar, and glucose in a pan and bring slowly to a boil. Remove from the heat, stir in the tea powder, and stir until dissolved (or if using leaves just stir), remove from the heat, and leave to infuse until cold, then strain. Transfer to an ice-cream maker and freeze according to the manufacturer's instructions. Place in a container and freeze until required.

For the banana tofu fool, place the tofu in a food processor and blend until smooth, then add the soy milk and vanilla extract and transfer to a bowl. Place the yogurt, chopped banana, lemon zest, and juice in the food processor and blend until smooth. Fold the banana mixture into the tofu mixture and then spoon it into the serving dishes. Refrigerate to set for up to 4 hours.

For the chocolate sauce, break up the chocolate and place in a small pan with the cream and vanilla extract. Warm it gently, stirring lightly until smooth and creamy, then remove and leave to cool.

To serve, place a ball of green tea sherbet on the top of the fool, spoon over the chocolate sauce, and decorate with mint.

Iced ricotta parfait
with caramelized bell peppers

I first saw sweet bell peppers being used in a dessert in New York some years ago. Chef David Burke of the Avenue Park Café in New York prepared an orange and strawberry tart with caramelized bell peppers for us—it was wonderful and a novel way of using them in a dessert preparation.

for the iced ricotta parfait

1/4 cup superfine sugar

2 free-range eggs, separated

1 vanilla bean, split lengthwise, seeds removed
    and reserved

1 cup heavy cream

1/4 pound ricotta cheese

1/3 cup Frangelico liqueur

zest of 1 lemon

hazelnut brittle (see PG TIPS)—optional

for the caramelized peppers

1 small red bell pepper, deseeded and cut
    into 1/3 inch dice

1 yellow bell pepper, deseeded and cut into 1/3 inch dice

4 tablespoons honey

1 teaspoon balsamic vinegar

juice of 1/2 lemon

1/4 cup soaked raisins, drained and dried

3 fresh tarragon leaves, chopped

6–8 small ramekins, soufflé dishes, or 8 metal kitchen rings

serves 6–8

For the parfait (best made a day in advance), whisk together the sugar, egg yolks, and vanilla seeds in a bowl until pale and almost doubled in volume. Half whip the cream until soft peaks begin to form (do not overwhisk). In another bowl, whisk the egg whites until very stiff peaks form. Add the cheese, liqueur, and lemon zest to the egg yolks and blend together. Gently fold in the whipped cream, then fold in the egg whites. Spoon the mixture into 6–8 chosen dishes. Cover with plastic wrap and freeze until required—at least 3 hours.

For the peppers, place them in a small pan with the honey and lightly caramelize them for 3–4 minutes until soft and tender. Add the vinegar, lemon juice, raisins, and tarragon and cook together for 5 minutes to form a light syrup. Remove from the heat and leave to cool. To serve, remove the parfaits from their molds by quickly immersing them halfway up in hot water, then turn them out onto individual serving plates. Leave to soften for 5 minutes. Pour the pepper syrup over the parfaits and serve immediately. Decorate with the nut brittle, if desired.

PG TIPS A simply prepared nut brittle makes a nice contrast to the parfait. Simply spread 3 tablespoons of peeled and chopped hazelnuts out on a lightly oiled cookie sheet. Combine 1/2 cup superfine sugar with 2 tablespoons of water in a pan and stir over a moderate heat until the sugar is dissolved. Bring to a boil and cook without stirring, until caramelized and golden. Remove from the heat, allow the bubbles to subside, and pour over the hazelnuts. Set aside to harden and go cold. When hard, roughly crush the pieces. This brittle can be made and stored successfully in an airtight container for 1 week.

Gooseberry clafoutis
with black olive ice cream

Ever since I first experienced sweet syrupy cooked olives in the south of
France some years ago, there has been no stopping my imagination
running riot. Here the candied olives are made into an unusual ice cream,
which contrasts beautifully with the warm clafoutis.

for the black olive ice cream

1/4 pound pitted black olives

1/2 cup sugar

1 cup milk

1 1/2 cups heavy cream

6 free-range egg yolks

for the gooseberry clafoutis

2 free-range eggs

2 free-range egg yolks

1/3 cup superfine sugar

2 tablespoons cornstarch

1/2 cup milk

1 cup heavy cream

1/2 vanilla bean, seeds removed and reserved

1/2 stick unsalted butter, melted

zest of 1/2 lemon

1 pound slightly underripe gooseberries

little confectioner's sugar to dust

Prepare the olive ice cream a day in advance. Cook the olives for 5 minutes in boiling water and then drain. Repeat this process three times to remove any bitterness from the olives and then chop finely. Place 1/2 cup sugar along with 2/3 cup water in a pan and slowly bring to a boil, raise the heat, add the chopped olives, and cook for about 10 minutes until jam-like in consistency. Remove and set aside.

Preheat the oven to 350°F. Heat the milk and cream in a pan along with the candied olives until almost boiling point, leave to infuse over a low heat without boiling for 10 minutes. Beat the egg yolks and remaining sugar in a bowl until light and fluffy, then gradually whisk the olive cream into the egg mixture. Return to the pan, stirring constantly over a low heat until the mixture thickens sufficiently to coat the back of a spoon. Do not let it boil or it will curdle. Remove from the heat and, when cool, refrigerate, then freeze in an ice-cream machine according to the manufacturer's instructions.

For the gooseberry clafoutis, place the eggs, egg yolks, and 2 tablespoons of sugar in a bowl and beat until light. Gradually add the cornstarch and beat to a smooth batter. Add the milk, cream, vanilla seeds, and 2 tablespoons of melted butter. Beat again until smooth. Put the remaining melted butter and sugar in a pan, add the gooseberries, lemon zest, and 1/2 cup water and cook for 8–10 minutes or until the gooseberries are just soft. Divide the gooseberries among four gratin-style dishes and then pour over an equal amount of the batter into each dish. Place in the oven to cook for 20–25 minutes until golden but still light and soft inside. Dust with confectioner's sugar and serve with the black olive ice cream.

Honey-roasted fruits
with rosemary and pear rosti

This is an ideal fruit dessert for the colder months. The fruits absorb the flavors of honey and rosemary as they cook, giving off a wonderful aroma which pervades the room. Serve with some crème fraîche mixed with some fresh vanilla seeds or extract.

for the pear rosti

2 pears

3 tablespoons maple syrup

2 egg yolks

3 tablespoons ground semolina

1 tablespoon unsalted butter

3 tablespoons superfine sugar

3 tablespoons unsalted butter

3 tablespoons whole blanched almonds

5 tablespoons clear honey

6 ounces seedless white grapes (preferably Muscat)

6 ounces dried apricots, soaked in water for 1 hour
   and drained

$^1/4$ pound dried prunes, soaked in water for 1 hour
   and drained

3 tablespoons cognac

juice of $^1/2$ lemon

1 teaspoon chopped fresh rosemary (plus a little more
   to decorate)

vanilla crème fraîche (optional)

For the pear rosti, peel the pears, remove the cores, and grate them coarsely. Dry in a cloth to squeeze out all the juice. Place in a bowl and add the syrup, egg yolks, and ground semolina to the pear. Mix well together and shape into four flat cakes. Melt the butter and fry the rosti until golden on both sides. Keep warm.

In a small skillet, heat the sugar with 1 teaspoon of water for about 5 minutes, until melted and golden. Whisk in half of the butter, add the almonds, and cook until caramelized in the sugar. Remove the almonds and set aside.

Melt the remaining butter in another larger skillet, add the honey, and bring to a boil. Add the grapes, apricots, and prunes and coat them evenly. Add the cognac and carefully ignite. Once the flames die out, add the lemon juice and rosemary and simmer gently until the sauce thickens.

Place one pear rosti in each dessert bowl, pour around the fruits, and sprinkle over the caramelized almonds. Garnish each with some rosemary and a good dollop of vanilla crème fraîche, if desired. Serve immediately.

Spice-roasted nectarines
with pistachio milk sauce

A refreshing dessert packed with flavor, ideal for the hot summer months when nectarines are ripe, juicy, and plentiful.

4 large firm but ripe nectarines

3 tablespoons unsalted butter

10 black peppercorns, cracked

1/2 teaspoon Szechuan peppercorns

1/2 teaspoon dried pink peppercorns

1/2 teaspoon ground star anise

2 tablespoons superfine sugar

2 tablespoons kirsch

for the pistachio milk sauce

1 small can condensed milk

2 tablespoons peeled pistachios

1 tablespoon kirsch

4 scoops of good quality vanilla ice cream

Preheat the oven to 450°F. Cut the nectarines in half, twist and separate, and remove the center stones. To remove the skins, place in a pan of boiling water for about 4 minutes—the skins will start to wrinkle and fall off. Remove the skins and place the nectarine halves in an ovenproof baking dish.

Melt the butter in a nonstick skillet, add the spices and cook for 1 minute. Add the sugar and 1/2 cup water and lightly caramelize together; add the kirsch. Pour the syrup over the nectarines and place in the oven to roast for 5–6 minutes.

Meanwhile for the sauce, place the condensed milk, pistachios, and kirsch in a food processor and blend until smooth.

To serve, pour a little pool of pistachio sauce in the center of each serving plate or shallow bowl, add two nectarine halves, top with 1 scoop of ice cream, and pour over the pan syrup.

Sauces and broths

As with all good cooking, perfection lies in getting the basic techniques right, none more so than when using a vegetable stock in a recipe. Poorly made vegetable broth can taste like dishwater and lack body and depth of flavor. Here are the stock and sauce bases used for this book that will help you ensure success every time. For those people who find brothmaking a tedious job, using a vegetable broth cube is fine, but some can be a little salty in flavor—take time to taste them madeup before use.

Light vegetable broth for soups and sauces

little olive oil

6 large carrots, peeled and sliced

4 stalks of celery, chopped

2 leeks, chopped

3 large onions, chopped

2 heads of garlic, halved horizontally

1 large turnip, chopped

small bunch of fresh flat-leaf parsley

small bunch of fresh thyme

small bunch of fresh cilantro

2 bay leaves

8 black peppercorns

8 pints water

makes 4 pints

Heat a very large heavy-based pan with a little olive oil, add the vegetables, cover with a lid, and sweat for 5 minutes. Add the herbs and spices, cover with water, and simmer gently for 40–45 minutes or until the vegetables are soft. Strain carefully through a fine strainer, leave to cool, and store until needed.

Roasted vegetable broth for sauce bases

2 ounces dried wild mushrooms (or fresh mushrooms)

4 large shallots, chopped

2 red bell peppers, deseeded and chopped

6 large carrots, peeled and chopped

2 leeks, chopped

2 garlic cloves, halved horizontally

little olive oil

2 tablespoons tomato paste

small bunch of fresh thyme

1 pound canned tomatoes, chopped

8 pints water

makes 4 pints

Preheat the oven to 425°F. Divide the mushrooms, shallots, bell peppers, carrots, leeks, and garlic between two large roasting pans. Drizzle a little olive oil over the vegetables and toss them well to ensure an even coating. Place in the oven to roast and lightly caramelize for about 30 minutes, turning them regularly as they roast. Remove, stir in a little tomato paste into each pan of vegetables, mix well, and return to the oven for a further 10 minutes. Remove and transfer to a large pan, add the thyme, chopped tomatoes, and cover with water. Simmer for 40 minutes. Strain carefully through a fine strainer, leave to cool, and store until needed.

Roasted vegetable reduction (vegetarian jus or vegetarian wine sauce)

4 tablespoons olive oil

$1/2$ stick unsalted butter

4 shallots, chopped

2 carrots, peeled and chopped

4 stalks of celery, chopped

6 garlic cloves, halved horizontally

1 pound button mushrooms, chopped

sprig of fresh thyme

1 tablespoon tomato paste

2 tablespoons all-purpose flour

$1/2$ cup red wine

8 pints roasted vegetable broth (see above)

1 tablespoon vegetarian Worcestershire sauce

$1^1/4$ cups Madeira or sherry

makes 4 pints

Heat the olive oil and butter in a large heavy-based pan, add the shallots, carrots, celery, and garlic and cook over a low heat for about 10–15 minutes until golden and lightly caramelized. Add the mushrooms and thyme and cook for a further 2–3 minutes. Stir in the tomato paste, cook for 1 minute, then mix in the flour and cook over a low heat for 2 minutes. Pour over the red wine, roasted vegetable broth, and Worcestershire sauce, stir, and bring to a boil. Add the Madeira, simmer for 20 minutes and then strain into a clean bowl, discarding the vegetables. Leave to cool and store until needed.

This sauce may be varied by changing the wine used, such as marsala or white wine. This sauce should be finished with a knob of butter before serving, which not only adds richness but also a wonderful shiny gloss to the sauce.

Index

Aduki beans
  pumpkin and aduki bean biryani, 97
Almonds
  almond crumble, 92
  chilled avocado and almond milk guacamole, 65
  green peppercorn ajo-blanco, 70
  salsa all'agresto, 131
  smoked almond dukkah, 147
Apples
  kadaifi apple fritters, 172
Apricots
  apricot relish, 30
  salad of chickpeas, cauliflower, and apricots, 84
Artichokes
  crushed artichoke and chèvre pesto toasts, 17
  stuffed Riesling-braised artichokes, 36
Asparagus
  Chinese-fried, 33
  pan-roasted asparagus, 29
  roasted tomato, chèvre, and asparagus salad, 72
  salad of hearts of palm, beet, and asparagus, 77
Avocados
  avocado cheese, 22
  avocado cream, 78
  avocado salsa rolls, 39
  chilled avocado and almond milk guacamole, 65
  vegetables à la Grecque, 22

Bananas
  banana tofu fool, 181
  tomato and banana pickle, 135
Basil
  basil puree, 72
  basil yogurt, 67
  Thai basil oil, 58
Beets
  beet caponata, 46
  beet gazpacho, 63
  beet raita, 136
  cream cheese, beet, and truffle tarts, 18
  parsnip tatin with pickled beets, 167
  salad of hearts of palm, beet, and asparagus, 77
  summer ruby salad, 83
  truffled beet salad, 117
Bitter greens
  crushed potato and bitter greens cannelloni, 113
Black beans
  avocado salsa rolls, 39
  black bean piperade, 138
  Cajun black bean soup, 56
  hot eggplant pasta, 123
Bombay tortillas, 144
Bread salad, 155
Broad bean crostini salad, 76
Broths
  light vegetable broth, 188
  roasted vegetable broth, 188
Bubble and squeak frittata, 145
Buckwheat spaetzle, 100
Butternut squash
  butternut squash and blue cheese tacos, 148
  cumin-roasted squash salad, 73
  toasted butternut squash and chèvre risotto, 92

Cabbage
  bubble and squeak frittata, 145
Cajun black bean soup, 56
Cajun mozzarella and ricotta fritters, 12
Carrots
  carrot pachadi, 24
  celeriac and carrot remoulade, 166
  haloumi tandoori, 24
  Sardinian carrot gnocchi, 104
  spiced carrot soup, 55
Cashew nuts
  cashew kibbeh crust, 149
  cashew pesto, 153
Cauliflower
  cauliflower and date tagine, 128
  cauliflower singaras, 169
  salad of chickpeas, cauliflower, and apricots, 84
Celeriac
  celeriac and carrot remoulade, 166
  grated celeriac, camembert, and prune tarts, 160
  twice-baked macaroni and celeriac soufflé, 124
Cheese
  avocado cheese, 22
  broad bean crostini salad, 76
  butternut squash and blue cheese tacos, 148
  Cajun mozzarella and ricotta fritters, 12
  cheese and tomato French toasts, 37
  cheese cracknel, 38
  cream cheese panna cotta, 180
  cream cheese, beet, and truffle tarts, 18
  crushed artichoke and goat's cheese pesto toasts, 17
  eggplant and cheese croquettes, 142
  feta cheese custard, 150
  chèvre and polenta tart, 162
  grated celeriac, camembert, and prune tarts, 160
  grilled paneer cheese, 155
  haloumi tandoori, 24
  iced ricotta parfait, 183
  open-faced spinach and feta sambusak, 174
  pickled blue cheese salad, 172
  roasted tomato, chèvre, and asparagus salad, 72
  roquefort-stuffed fig salad, 78
  rosemary-broiled chèvre, 30
  smoked paprika feta salad, 86
  tagliatelle with creamy brie, 122
  toasted butternut squash and chèvre risotto, 92

  torta di scalogni, 163
  vegetables à la Grecque, 22
  vine-basked camembert, 32
  wild mushroom and tallegio croque monsieurs, 17
  zaatar crushed labna, 47
Cheesecake
  lavender yogurt cheesecake, 178
Cherry jus, 95
Chickpeas
  Goan chickpea risotto, 96
  salad of chickpeas, cauliflower, and apricots, 84
  stuffed zucchini flowers, 27
Chicory
  tagliatelle with caramelized chicory, 121
Chocolate dressing, 73
Chocolate sauce, 181
Coconut
  coconut yogurt, 135
  sweet potato and coconut polenta, 106
Coriander chutney, 169
Corn
  buttermilk corn bisque, 61
  mango and corn salsa, 156
  Swiss chard and corn crespelle, 130
Couscous
  cumin and fig couscous, 98
  saffron couscous, 152
Cream cheese
  cream cheese, beet, and truffle tarts, 18
  cream cheese panna cotta, 180
Cucumber
  cool cucumber soup, 60
Cumin
  cumin and fig couscous, 98
  cumin-roasted squash salad, 73
  cumin spinach, 134
Curry
  curry paste, 60
  green jungle curry, 141
  Kerala pumpkin curry, 136

Daikon
  seaweed daikon wraps, 25
Dates
  cauliflower and date tagine, 128

Eggplants
  eggplant and cheese croquettes, 142
  eggplant and tomato rolls, 41
  eggplant kiibbeh, 40
  grilled baby eggplant salad, 75
  hot eggplant pasta, 123
  Mediterranean pisto pie, 165
  mini eggplant egg rolls, 13
Eggs
  black bean piperade, 138
  bubble and squeak frittata, 145
  egg salad, 85
  poached eggs on potato muffins, 28
  quail's eggs béarnaise tartlets, 171

Fennel
  fennel and zucchini osso bucco, 152

  fennel salsa, 32
  fennel soup, 57
  Jerusalem artichoke, bean, and fennel salad, 70
Fettucini with nettles, 122
Figs
  cumin and fig couscous, 98
  roquefort-stuffed fig salad, 78
Fregola
  Sardinian carrot gnocchi, 104
French string beans
  French string bean and shallot vinaigrette, 37
  Jerusalem artichoke, bean, and fennel salad, 70
  red tofu salad, 74
Fruit
  fruit ceviche soup, 58
  honey-roasted fruits, 185

Garlic
  garlic butter, 122
  garlic truffle cream, 38
  parsley and garlic sauce, 175
  rolled wild garlic and pumpkin lasagne, 112
Ginger and sesame dipping sauce, 25
Gnocchi
  purple potato gnocchi, 105
  Sardinian carrot gnocchi, 104
Goan chickpea risotto, 96
Gooseberry clafoutis, 184
Greek-stuffed onions, 150
Green jungle curry, 141
Green peppercorn ajo-blanco, 70
Green tea sherbet, 181
Gremolata, 29
  castelli, 152

Honey-roasted fruits, 185
Honey-roasted vegetables, 98

Iced ricotta parfait, 183

Jerusalem artichoke, bean, and fennel salad, 70

Kadaifi apple fritters, 172
Keftedes, 133
Kerala pumpkin curry, 136

Lasagne
  lasagne salad, 81
  rolled wild garlic and pumpkin lasagne, 112
Lavender
  lavender oil, 72
  lavender yogurt cheesecake, 178
Leeks
  caramelized, 104
  potato and leek flamiche, 166
  Spanish romescu baby leeks, 35
Lemons
  deep-fried lemon zest, 121
  lemon olive oil, 27
  preserved lemon salsa, 175
Lentils
  lentil vinaigrette, 160
  puy lentil bouillabaise, 64